Unwin Education Books: 9

LEARNING IN THE PRIMARY SCHOOL

Unwin Education Books

Education since 1800 IVOR MORRISH
Moral Development WILLIAM KAY
Physical Education for Teaching BARBARA CHURCHER
The Background of Immigrant Children IVOR MORRISH
Organizing and Integrating the Infant Day JOY TAYLOR
Education: Its Nature and Purpose M. V. C. JEFFREYS
Learning in the Primary School KENNETH HASLAM

Unwin Education Books: 9
Series Editor: Ivor Morrish

Learning in the Primary School

KENNETH R. HASLAM
Headmaster, Brockworth County Primary School Gloucestershire

London
GEORGE ALLEN AND UNWIN LTD
RUSKIN HOUSE MUSEUM STREET

First published 1971

ISBN 0 04 371017 4 *Cased*
ISBN 0 04 371018 2 *Paper*

Printed in Great Britain
in 10pt. on 12pt. Times Roman
by Billing & Sons Limited
Guildford and London

Preface

This book was prompted by what the author considers to be a need amongst young teachers and would-be teachers for suggestions of a very practical nature to help in the management of a class or group of primary school children. It is not intended to be a means of persuasion towards any particular type of approach or method of organization, but rather an attempt to narrow the gap between theory and practice; in fact, a continuation of the process of learning to be a successful and effective teacher.

There has been no attempt to deal in great detail with any subject, because to do so would be an impossible task in a book of this size, the field of study for the primary school teacher being so wide.

This book, therefore, merely scratches the surface of many problems and approaches, but it is hoped that the suggestions and ideas will help the new teacher to overcome initial difficulties and perhaps encourage others to experiment.

Contents

Illustrations

Introduction

The task of the good teacher is to help others to learn. Consequently, of prime importance is the organization of children's activities in such a way that each child is working at his own level and is finding enough to interest and challenge him.

Children do not all share the same mental capacity and as a result they are unable to absorb instructions and to complete a given piece of work in the same time and with equal efficiency. What arrangements should be made for the more advanced children who are capable of working with such speed and accuracy? How can we cope with the slower learner? How can effective learning be promoted at all levels? The answers are not simple and straightforward, nor is there any panacea for all difficulties.

You, as a person responsible for the education of perhaps a group of thirty or forty youngsters, will not go far wrong if you constantly remind yourself that each child is an individual, with his peculiar emotional, intellectual and social problems. He is also a member of a group and as such will benefit from contact with others socially, and in the learning situation.

Many teachers have come to the conclusion, later confirmed by practice, that the most efficient method of organization is to arrange their pupils to work with the whole class occasionally, in smaller groups of four or six more often, and usually in pairs or singly. Well organized classrooms are attractive and inviting, and the work arranged for the children to do is stimulating and suited to each particular child. Materials are purposefully arranged and made readily available for use.

An efficient teacher will be anxious to help children with their reading difficulties, to diagnose problems, and to promote an interest in books. Mathematics will be meaningful and structured to meet individual needs; and advantage will be taken of the environment in its use as a basis for projects and other studies.

Although a teacher of primary school children can and should make use of his own special interests and abilities, he will be a teacher of integrated subjects and therefore aware of teaching techniques in many fields. A good teacher must be able to develop suitable contacts with parents so that he and they can watch and nurture children's progress. A good school and the home are complementary to each other, the organization of the school being such that it can cater for children coming from a variety of home environments. The cooperation between school and home can therefore be of immense value in helping the child to develop not only correct attitudes to learning, but the moral and spiritual values necessary for a well-balanced individual.

Chapter 1

Classroom and Group Organization

A THE ENVIRONMENT

The environment into which the children come each day is very important. You, of course, will be primarily concerned with that of your classroom, but you may find opportunities elsewhere, for example, immediately beyond your teaching area, where you can be effective. A bare room, containing only chairs and desks, can be very lifeless. On the other hand, a room full of interesting things, tastefully arranged, to see, touch and experience, can be a very exciting and stimulating place. You could begin by introducing a few pictures related to subjects you intend to talk about, or to a particular season of the year. You could bring initially, some flowers or other nature specimens to put on a table for display. Very soon, with a little persuasion, the children will be bringing pictures and specimens of their own. The writer recalls a particularly attractive corner of one classroom where autumn fruits were displayed. The wall background was covered with various shades of coloured tissue paper with browns and reds, yellows and gold. Here and there were autumn leaves, twigs, and pictures carefully mounted. Soon, children's leaf prints, poems and written descriptions were added; and the acorns which disappeared, to be used as counters or weights for science, were replenished the next day.

Another important corner is the one where the class or group library is kept. More will be said about the use of the library, but in the context of classroom arrangement, this should take pride of place. Books should be readily accessible and attractively displayed. The library must be inviting; it should be a place where a child can sit, preferably at a small table or desk, to browse or to search for information. A vase of flowers on top of the shelves or on the table will make the area much more attractive.

No classroom is complete without a living creature of some kind, for the children to handle, feed or just observe. At the very least, try to have a goldfish in a tank (not a bowl, which is too small and does not have enough surface exposed to the air). Other suggestions are: a bird, a hamster, a guinea-pig, white mice, a rabbit (this is probably better outside in a large cage); the possibilities are almost endless.

It is very desirable to have on display items of mathematics equipment that the children will need to have available for use at any time. Material hidden away in cupboards tends to be neglected or forgotten. Structural apparatus, lengths of string and tape, things for counting, measuring apparatus for capacity, length, weight, time, and money: all should be to hand.

No doubt from time to time you will want to lay out musical instruments, or a composite model made by a group of children, or items of interest brought by different people. You will not be able to display all of these at once, but bear them in mind, because it is a good plan to change the material on display frequently in order to produce a fresh and thereby continued interest.

In addition to models and other items created by the children, it is very encouraging for them to have their written work displayed, often on the walls, though booklets can be placed on tables or hung on string. Poems, descriptive writing, accounts of experiences or visits, can and should be constantly shown. Avoid putting up only the best work; give credit for a good effort, thus enabling even the dullest child to have something to display. Bear in mind a child's limitations but never accept his inferior work.

With a little ingenuity and thought your displays can be very attractive and worth-while. And from you the children will learn. They should be encouraged to be discriminating but you must first show them what is beautiful and attractive.

A word or two about materials for display would be appropriate. A profusion of large drawing-pins can be ugly. Some now available have small heads in a variety of colours, white being the most versatile. Try ordinary dressmaking pins forced into a display board with a 'rampin', or you could try opening out a paper stapler and using the staples as pins. A picture rarely looks good without a frame, so why not take the trouble to cut out a shape slightly larger than the picture from a piece of sugar paper or card? An alternative would be simply to have available several different lengths of card or thick paper about 4 to 6 cm wide from which frames could easily be made. Also, there is a plastic material available, rather like plasticine, a small ball of which will stick pictures to almost any surface; it can be used repeatedly.

You and the children will be spending many hours in and around your classroom or teaching area, so make it as pleasant and as attractive as you can.

B MATERIALS FOR THE TEACHER

There are several items which are really a teacher's stock-in-trade. Although many teachers, particularly in primary schools, are using the blackboard less frequently, you will still require a good deal of chalk, not only white but various colours. There is a dustless variety which is a little more expensive but well worth the extra cost. Try to obtain a good supply of felt-tipped pens of different colours. These are handy for illustrations and titles for displays. Ball-point pens are useful because, unlike pencils, they do not require constant sharpening. Transparent cellulose tape is invaluable for many jobs but it is better to avoid its use when repairing borrowed library books – frowned upon by most librarians – and on walls where it may loosen paint from plaster. Ask for a good, large, pair of scissors and if possible a stapler. If you can, have an odds-and-ends box containing needle and cotton, tape, paper fasteners, pins, etc.

Many teachers like to make their own collections of books and pictures. From time to time you will discover books and pamphlets which will help you with your teaching, and which can often be a source of information or inspiration, so adding to the effectiveness of your lessons. Sometimes you will recall a poem or a piece of description in one of the books on your personal shelf. Pictures and other illustrations, catalogued for easy reference, are of great help to a teacher and are often more effective than a wordy description.

You will no doubt be required to keep a record book, but the approach to this is so varied that no comment is made here. However, you will find that a personal note book, particularly in your early teaching career, is very useful. Teaching notes, suitable poems, sources of stories, and general information could be listed for easy reference. You may also wish to indicate children's progress and details of work covered. Record keeping is mentioned in Chapter 9.

C ORGANIZATION OF MATERIALS FOR THE CHILDREN'S USE

There is a very wide range of materials available and your use of them will vary according to the needs of the children in your care. Perhaps comments about some of them would be appropriate.

Pencils

Thicker ones for younger infants are better, usually 'B', so that they can make large black letters and figures. A thinner 'HB' is better for older children who are able to exercise more manipulative skill. Older children can usually manage to sharpen their own pencils if you have one or two sharpeners available – avoid knives because they can be dangerous and do not do as neat a job. Be aware of the youngster who, just for the joy of sharpening his pencil, frequently breaks the point deliberately. When the children are responsible for their own pencils, a small slice cut at an angle about half an inch from the blunt end will give you a suitable surface on which to write a child's name. It is perhaps better with younger children to have a box of sharpened pencils available so that, should a point break during a lesson, that pencil can be exchanged for another without any interruption of what might be an interesting piece of work. This also leaves the teacher free to help others. The broken points are then sharpened at an appropriate time during the day.

Erasers

Avoid their over-use by keeping a few on your table for collection when needed.

Pens

The policy laid down by the school will decide what type of pen is to be used by the older children. Some schools allow ball-point pens for speed of working; others dislike them because of possible smudging. Few schools still use very fine nibs, which are difficult to manage with any speed; some like an italic or rounded nib with attached reservoir, to save blots and constant dipping in inkwells for a fresh supply of ink. Some schools prefer the children to use their own fountain-pens as soon as possible; good ones, moderately priced with replaceable nibs, are available, and providing reasonable care is taken of them, they should last a long time. It is always worth-while to buy good quality ink, especially for fountain-pens, and a large bottle or can available for class use is better than small bottles kept by children in their desks – you will realize why after the first spill over precious books! An alternative, when ordinary pens are used, is to fill inkwells from a gallon can with good quality ink. You may like to try the different colours of blue, blue-black, and black. The last looks particularly good on decorative or illustrative work.

Coloured pencils, crayons and felt pens

In the early stages, thick wax crayons are better for infants to manage, but soon they will be able to cope with the thinner type. Indeed, they will require these as their ability to control the implement improves and they find the need to be more precise and to include more detail. Greater accuracy can be obtained with pencil crayons which have to be sharpened. Some teachers provide the children with coloured felt-tipped pens which are very effective for designs and patterns.

Paper

Various kinds of paper in different sheet sizes should be to hand. These include scrap paper, lined paper for older children, and plain sheets for art and craft, making booklets or writing. It is also worthwhile to investigate the different qualities of papers and to have a varied selection available. Remember that children usually prefer a large surface area for painting and illustration, so do not restrict them to tiny pieces of paper. Those who have not had the opportunity to use large areas of paper tend to limit themselves to one corner and to do tiny pictures.

Other art and craft materials

Some teachers store paints away in cupboards or in specially provided stock rooms. You will probably find it an advantage to have a table holding a few paint brushes and paints, crayons, scissors, various sizes and kinds of art paper, etc., so that children can use them at any convenient or appropriate time during the day. An illustration in a booklet, folder, or even an exercise book does not always have to be coloured by crayon alone; and certainly part of the joy of producing a personal folder or booklet is in the actual making, by scoring, folding and possibly stitching it, and illustrating the cover.

The most versatile type of paint is powder; it is easily dissolved and mixed to obtain variations in colour, and has a varying texture. Blocks of hard paint are easy to use and although not as effective as powder are less prone to be wasted. You may like to try plastic paints and even oils for older children.

Have available at least one kind of paste or gum. A small bottle of adhesive with a rubber mouth is useful for quick jobs; cold water-paste will readily stick large surfaces, particularly those of paper or thin card; and a paste with a rubber base has the advantage of being both versatile and easily removable from unwanted places by simply rubbing with the finger when dry.

Try some of the new materials which are put to good use in many classrooms now. Polystyrene in sheets or blocks can be fashioned and cut with a heated wire (a special tool can be bought quite cheaply) and will readily take paint; perspex is a versatile substance which can be bent into different shapes when heated slightly, and also sawn, drilled, sandpapered, and even planed; brilliant paints are very attractive to children and can be purchased through the main suppliers, together with varieties of the new modelling compounds now available; and much useful material can be procured from a joiner's shop, a junk yard, or even children's homes. A box containing an assortment of materials of various textures and colours would be helpful for making collages and models.

The materials mentioned should be easily accessible to the children and they should know where to find them, and be taught how to use them well. The lead in the middle of pencils might crack if dropped, and rulers cannot be used to draw straight lines when dented – obvious remarks but details which require pointing out.

Always have a generous supply of newspaper available, mainly for painting and pasting, but also for protecting the floor and tables. Thin plastic sheeting is also very useful for covering tables and desks and can readily be washed.

Children need to be taught how to keep the work area reasonably tidy, and how to clear away. There should be definite places for storing each item and a child should be aware that he is responsible for cleaning and storing paint brushes, paste brushes, palettes, etc. It is wise to appoint a rota of helpers who will be responsible for the general tidiness of art and craft materials and, in fact, for other classroom items. Although some children will always be willing to stay after the others have gone home, a sound plan is to begin clearing away in good time, otherwise you may be spending your valuable preparation time on tidying up! Spare a thought for the caretaker also. He usually prefers things to be off the floor and most surfaces free for dusting.

D CLASSROOM ARRANGEMENTS

Furniture should be arranged in such a way that there is space enough for children to walk about freely. This is not easy where the classroom is small and the numbers large, but there are certain ways of economizing on space. For instance, the arrangement of desks or tables in groups to accommodate six children is more space-saving than in groups for four. That is, in a class of thirty-six, six groups of six will leave more space than nine groups of four. Where

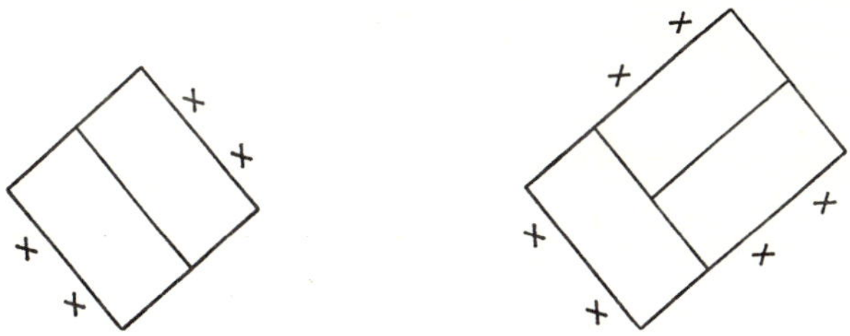

there is adequate light, the placing of desks or tables near a wall will help to give more free space in a crowded classroom.

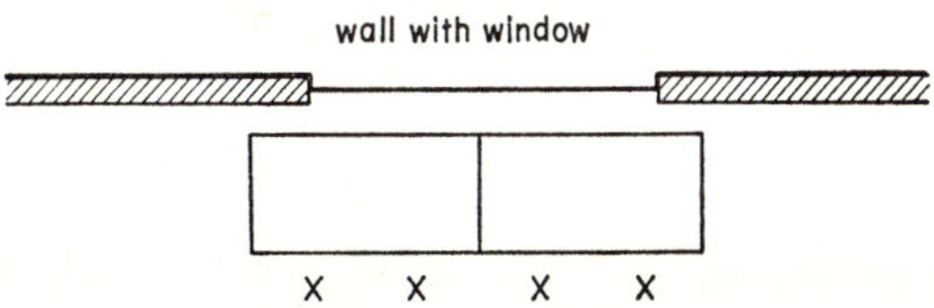

Where more room is available the teacher has the opportunity of arranging corners and small areas of display with the object of encouraging children to work in small groups or to seek a secluded corner in order to indulge in some quiet reading or personal study.

Some possible classroom layouts are given in diagrams 1, 2, and 3, but it must be emphasized that the variety of arrangements is limitless and that the grouping and placing of furniture and

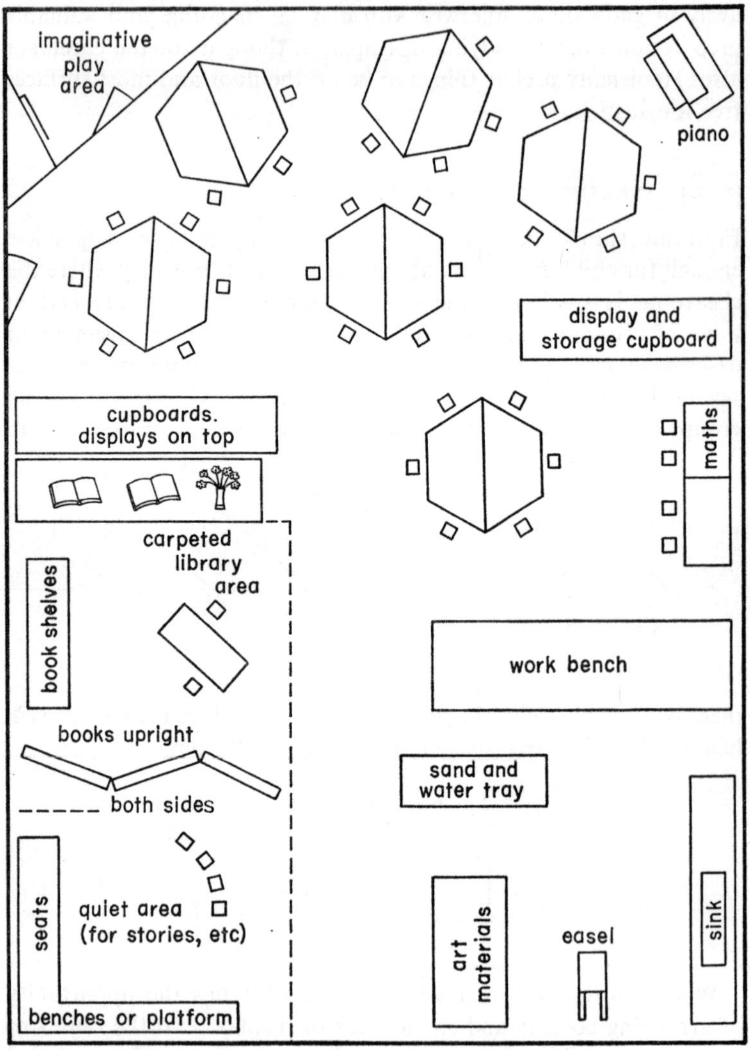

1. Suggested Layout of Classroom for Younger Infants.

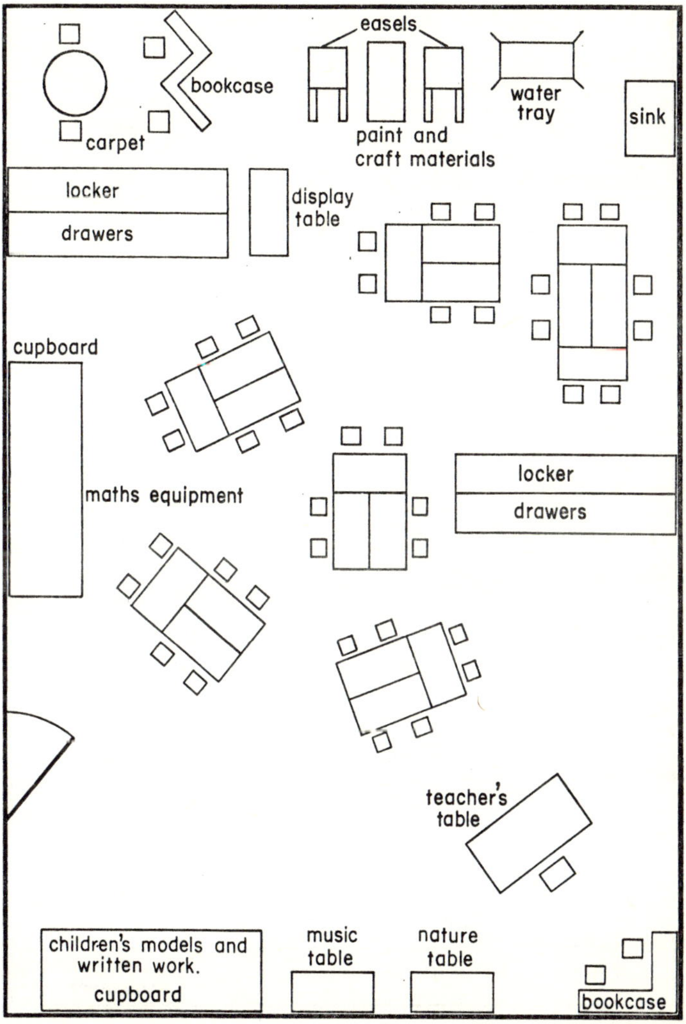

2. Suggested Layout of Classroom for Upper Infants or Lower Juniors.

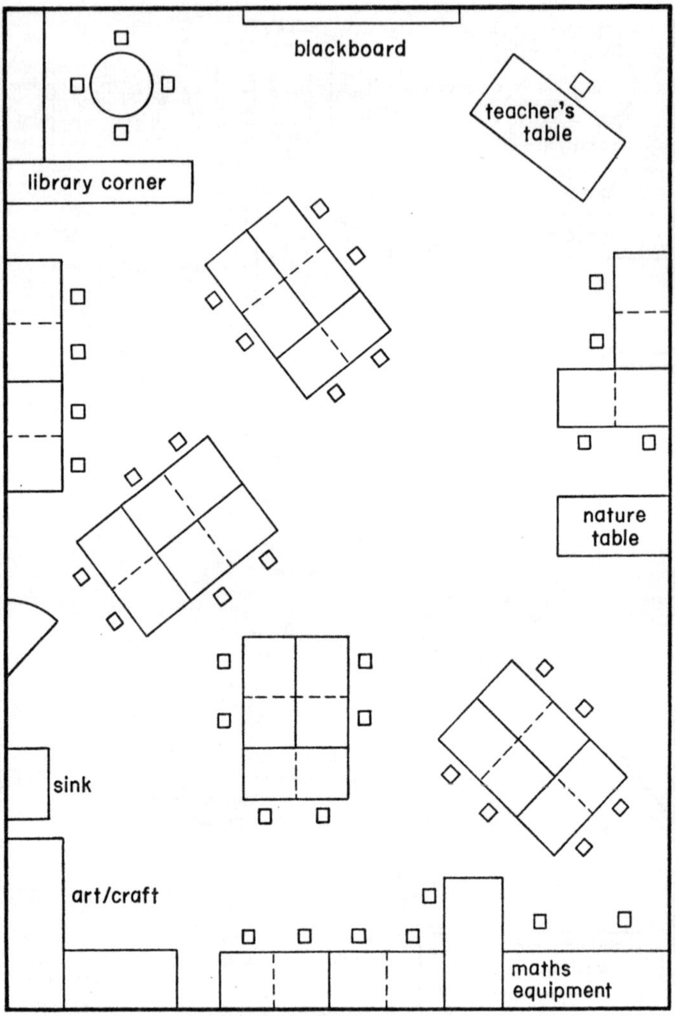

3. Suggested Layout of Classroom for Upper Juniors.

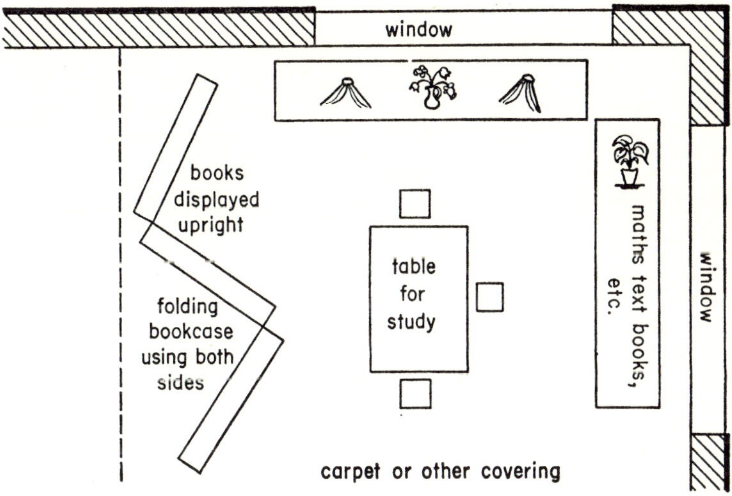

4. Library Area with Windows.

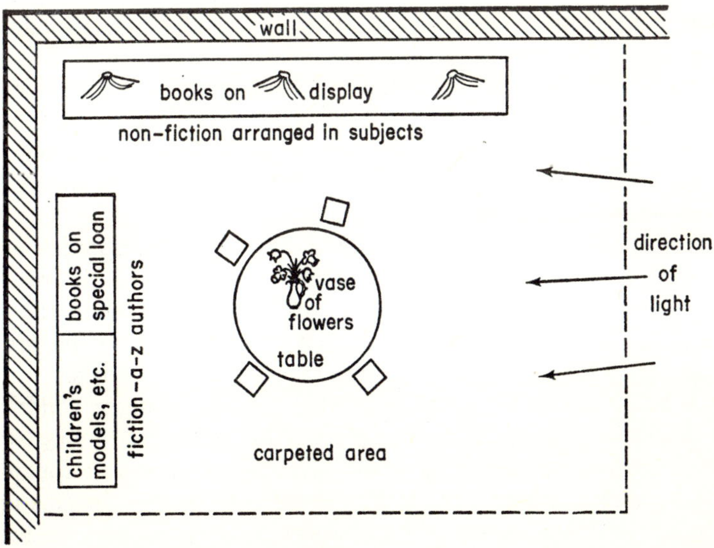

5. Library Area without Windows.

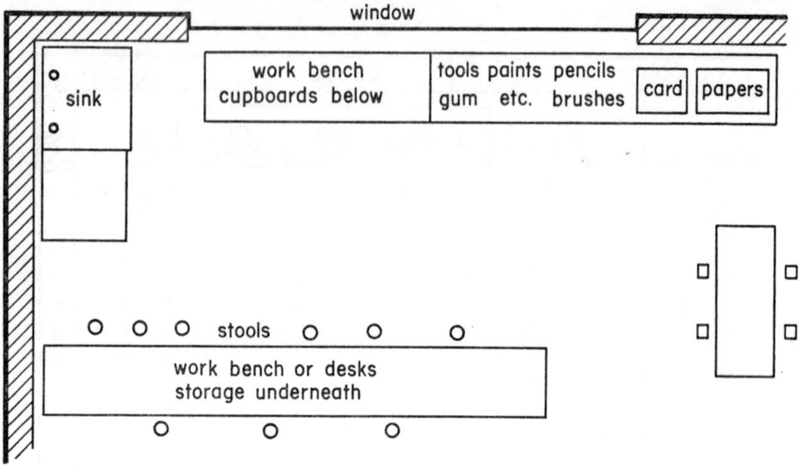

6. Art and Craft Area.

equipment must always be adapted to the needs of the children and to the policy of the school.

Diagrams 4 and 5 show suggested library corners or areas. Again, several adaptations could be tried. One wall should have a window if possible (diagram 4), but certainly there should be plenty of light coming from the direction of the arrows (diagram 5). Note the use of the tops of library shelves for displaying books and the occasional vase of flowers or plant placed here or there. Where carpeting is available the whole of a library area can be covered, providing a pleasant quiet place for reading.

An art and craft area is suggested in diagram 6. Art materials are laid out on a bench, making them readily available and the area is partially enclosed by having a work bench at right-angles to one of the walls. It is an advantage for this work bench to have cupboards underneath for storing paper, card and other craft materials.

A house corner or imaginative play area for younger children could also be carpeted, and if a corner of the room is used only two sides need to be erected. It is an advantage if these can contain a door and a window. Inside it is possible to have a dressing-up box full of materials, a table and chairs, a tea set, a bed, kitchen equipment, a doll and cradle. Parents will often help in providing these materials, and in making clothes for the children to be 'doctors', 'nurses', 'bus conductors', 'postmen' and 'housewives'.

E THE INTEGRATED DAY

A number of schools have purposely reduced to a minimum any schemes of work, timetable, class instruction, and even break times. This has come about because of a change of emphasis in the primary school from work that is 'subject centred' to that which is 'child centred'. Teachers have begun to consider in greater detail the child's intellectual, physical, emotional, and social needs, and have sought new ways of encouraging individual learning, motivated by discovery.

The idea that each child is to be treated as an individual and allowed to progress at his own rate, is expressed in socially accepted, unstreamed and, in some cases, vertically grouped classes; these highlight the important change from the situation, more teacher-imposed, in which the whole class is taught as a group, to that in which each child finds a variety of activities to stimulate him and uninterrupted time (within reason) to pursue his own interests.

Enlightened teachers already attempt to cater, in part, for these needs and have adapted their methods accordingly. Some have developed the idea still further and have adopted an 'integrated day'.

Integration, according to one dictionary explanation, is a 'combination of parts into a whole'. It follows therefore that to integrate a school day would be to combine its parts into one whole; in other words to treat it as a whole rather than follow a strict timetable of events.

If you are confronted with this situation in school, your first consideration is the classroom. Some arrangements of furniture and materials have already been discussed, but for the integrated day, it is necessary to have separate small work bays and for the room to be partitioned; this can be done by placing cupboards and work benches projecting from the walls, with some perhaps left in the centre of the room. Make sure that the entrance to the room is reasonably free and not cluttered with milk bottles or work that could easily be spoiled should someone brush against it. Arrange for activities requiring the use of the sink to be near to it, and for quiet areas such as the library, reading and maths. corners to be as far as possible from the woodwork bench or drama area. It is not essential for each child to have a particular desk which belongs to him, and in fact this would be difficult to ensure with these arrangements. It is important, however, for each child to have a locker or a drawer he can call his own.

All that has been said in a previous chapter about the importance of the classroom environment applies here. There must be material to stimulate interest and encourage experiment. The type of material will depend, of course, on the ages and abilities of the children. Avoid, however, providing such a variety of material that the children are at once overwhelmed and find difficulty in making their choice of activity. If you limit the amount and variety you will be able to keep a stock of materials available for frequent changes when there is a demand.

But, if the integrated day is new to you, be realistic. Approach the situation gradually and allow a few of the class at a time to have the freedom to investigate a limited amount of material you have put at their disposal. An infant classroom will have, for instance, a sand or water tray with various sizes of containers, tubes, funnels, and things that float; there will be structural apparatus for building, comparing, sorting, classifying, etc.; a screen will provide a 'house' for the younger ones to engage in imaginative play, and for the older ones to use as a drama area. Junior children can be provided with bulbs and batteries; magnets; materials for constructing shapes and models; structural, weighing and measuring apparatus for mathematics; musical instruments; clay; and in fact, anything from which a learning situation can develop.

There will be a considerable overlap between the materials provided for infants and those for juniors. Children will of course work at different levels. All should have art and craft materials and paper and pencils for writing readily available. Most important of all, and in fact essential for the successful organization and learning in any classroom, is the provision of a variety of suitable books. Obviously, no classroom or area can contain books giving information about every possible topic. This is where selection and limited choice are an advantage. If the material you provide will lead to investigations about, say, fossils or prehistoric animals, then you should borrow books on these subjects beforehand if possible, either from the school central library or from other class libraries. As mentioned in the chapter dealing with books, local county libraries also are suitable sources.

When a child is not used to being allowed a choice of activity, or if he has previously been subjected to the will of a dominating parent or teacher, he may constantly seek your guidance about what he should do. One method found to work quite well is to enlist the help of some others who show confidence in the way they tackle their work and attach the unsure child to them for a time. Another way, if the child can read, is to devise assignment cards, directing him to certain apparatus and suggesting different areas of exploration. It is important that these cards are written using a vocabulary easily understood by the children for whom they are particularly intended, and that the directions are clear. Moreover, to be successful they should not merely give directions, but should be a source of inspiration for further investigation (see Chapter 5).

Individual activities will usually have to stop for P.E., radio, television, French or singing. Also it is good for the children to listen to poetry or to hear a story together, often at the end of the day (vertically grouped classes could exchange age groups for this). At certain other times, you may find it advisable for the whole class to gather together to discuss what some of them have discovered or achieved so that a spirit of cooperation and encouragement is engendered.

Make sure that everyone knows where materials can be found, teach the care of tools, and train them how to clear away and leave the classroom tidy. Make these jobs mostly their responsibility, not yours.

The advantages of the learning situations created by the integrated day are obvious, but there are certain pitfalls to be avoided. Necessities such as a child's need for his own place, the limiting of activities, the gradual approach to prevent chaos, catering for the child who is unsure about what to do, the grouping of the class occasionally, and children's responsibilities have been discussed. The teacher should ensure that each child is progressing at his own pace and that he is finding sufficient challenges and stimulation.

> 'The sense of personal discovery influences the intensity of a child's experience, the vividness of his memory and the probability of effective transfer of learning. At the same time it is true that trivial ideas and inefficient methods may be "discovered". Furthermore, time does not allow children to find their way by discovery to all that they have to learn. In this matter, as in all education, the teacher is responsible for encouraging children in enquiries which lead to discovery and for asking leading questions.' (Children and Their Primary Schools – Plowden Report).

Two ideas will help. Firstly, have a plan of campaign. Write down what materials you intend to provide and what you expect the children will learn from them. These, of course, will have to be modified to allow for individual needs, and you will have to guide children's thoughts and actions along certain paths, by suggestions or reference to apparatus, assignment cards or books. Secondly, have detailed records of all children's work, difficulties, achievements, and if possible, social adjustment. Unless adequate written records are kept, the levels reached by all children will not be remembered and adequate progress cannot be planned. These records will be valuable when an assessment has to be given to the head teacher or parent, and will prove very helpful when a child moves to another teacher or school. Some samples of recording will be found in the chapter on mathematics, and these could be adapted for other subjects such as reading. Should you be required to make more comprehensive records, you will find suggestions in Chapter 9. Whether it is required or not, you would benefit from a record kept up to date weekly; a book or loose-leaf folder would be best for this, with a page allocated to each child. This could include remarks about happenings, further stages of development, health, etc., noted as comments with dates. Such a book would prove invaluable when writing end-of-term reports. It would also give you a sense of orderliness and help you to feel secure in what you are doing.

Chapter 2

Preparing for a New Class

If you are new to school, you will no doubt have made preliminary visits to ascertain generally what will be required of you and, more specifically, the details of your schemes of work, your timetable, and the ages and levels of ability of the children you will be teaching. The children will be as apprehensive as you and will need to be reassured that you are the kind of person who will be firm but kind, sympathetic to needs yet aware that children must learn to be independent, and fair in your decisions and judgements, appearing to treat everyone alike yet varying your relationships to suit the individual needs of each child.

This applies also to a teacher who has taught other classes in the same school, except that the class you receive will already have a good idea what to expect and the kind of things that please you and what you will or will not allow.

It is of great importance for you to bear in mind that each child has his own personality, home environment and relationships with those at school and at home. Some may be without one or both parents because of death, divorce or separation; some may have no brothers or sisters, others as many as ten or twelve. Some will come from homes with very little cultural background, where books are almost non-existent and conversation is limited to threats and sharp words of command; others will be blessed with all that you would consider good in life, and a home where there is cultural stimulation and an atmosphere of understanding and love.

In your class you can expect to find children of any of these types; in addition, children will also vary because of the differing degree of such factors in their environment, and the nature of their response.

Growing children are developing physically, mentally, and emotionally; all develop at different paces and are at different levels. To expect every child to respond effectively to one particular level of instruction or method of teaching would be to expect the impossible. Individual differences compel a good teacher to adopt flexible classroom approaches. Those children who are deprived of books, pictures and stimulating conversation at home are at a disadvantage and will have to be compensated at school if a well integrated personality is to result. Those who have an entirely opposite home background will require a more mature and extensive treatment to satisfy their needs. Most children, however, will fall somewhere between these two categories and it will be a major task for you to discover just where.

Many teachers express concern that they do not know what to expect from the children in their new class or what levels of work and understanding each child has achieved. The samples of work shown in Appendix I will give you some idea of the work of children at various ages. Consultation with the previous teacher of the class is invaluable. A short period of discussion will help you to ascertain capabilities and achievements. Of at least equal importance is information concerning the attitudes, temperaments, idiosyncrasies and home backgrounds of the children. There may be one child for whom the best scolding would be the length of your tongue, but another for whom a quiet word would be sufficient. One child may have far too much done for him at home and needs to be encouraged to have a little more self-reliance; while another may need your sympathetic care because he is short of parental affection. Record cards for these children will almost certainly be available for you to scrutinize.

Having ascertained what to expect from the children, your next job is to plan the kind of work you intend them to do. As already said, much will depend upon the schemes of work and how closely you will be expected to follow them. We will therefore purposely omit the content, and concentrate on general organization and methods of tackling learning situations.

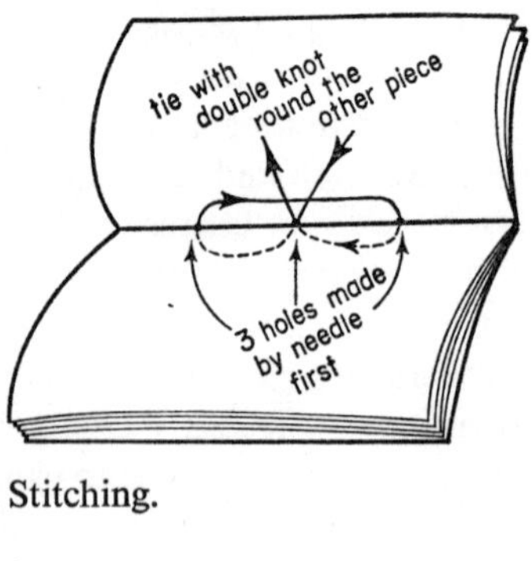

7. Simple Book Stitching.

General Organization

Each child will require a sharpened pencil (and a pen if ready for it) and a ruler. If you allow them to use an eraser, one each will encourage a lot of rubbing out, so have a couple on your desk; the definite effort of having to fetch and return it may discourage mistakes. It could, however, persuade some child that a little walk might relieve the tedium of the moment!

Books for the children to write in, or paper for them to use, will need to be at hand. Study the list of children's names and write them on at least one set of books or folders you have prepared. Paper is easier to display on the wall than a book, and can be kept in a folder; but books ensure that pages cannot get lost and can be considered as a compact whole. Try using both. Although you will want to use books of the commercially manufactured type some others could be made by you or the children. When they are made in the classroom, there is no necessity to adhere to any particular shape, size or thickness. A long, tall book may be very suitable for one purpose or topic while a short, fat one may be better for another. Thin art paper, folded several times with its edges cut by a guillotine and centre either stitched or stapled, can be made into an excellent book in a few minutes (see diagram 7).

Have sufficient paper and crayons available for all to use as one of your first activities if you have younger children. Older ones would probably appreciate choosing a library book or magazine, to read while you are attending to individual needs.

It is necessary that each child begins to feel, not only that you are aware of him and his requirements, but that he is needed as a member of the small community in which he finds himself. Monitors or helpers are an answer to this and they will also relieve you of much routine work. Try to include everyone, if not immediately then certainly at regular intervals, by using rotas. Helpers will be required for distributing milk, hymn books, pencils and other materials for general use, for doing messages, observing the weather, watering plants, attending to classroom animals, and for many other activities. Remember too that people are required for tidying up! You may also wish to have group leaders for the distribution of materials, and the co-ordination of groups within a class. Orderliness in a classroom is achieved not so much through teacher-imposed discipline, as through the organization of pencil supply, availability of materials and shared responsibility for everyday jobs. It is in the small details that we lay the foundations of the learning situation.

Chapter 3

Discipline and Behaviour

Part of what has been said in the last few pages really comes under the heading of discipline. Most people will agree that the ultimate goal is a child's self-discipline, achieved through an awareness of his social privileges and responsibilities and his concern for others beside himself. A child's introduction to social behaviour begins at home of course, where he learns first to please his parents and to share in the structure of family life. On his introduction to school he is required to conform to a certain routine, necessary for a happily organized community, and he seeks the approval and approbation of his teacher and immediate friends.

The teacher's task is to help the child to adjust himself to the classroom environment and to help him progress from actions motivated by a desire to please the teacher, to actions motivated by a sense of social obligation in relation to others, a desire to learn for the sheer joy and love of it, and a wish to prepare himself to be a responsible member of society.

If this is to be achieved, a good teacher–child relationship is essential. An overbearing teacher could prevent correct adjustment and inhibit a child's growth towards independence and self-confidence. It follows therefore that persuasion is preferable to forceful command, and where orders and directions are necessary, an accompanying explanation is in many circumstances desirable. The teacher must, however, make some aspects of his personality felt in the classroom. The children must feel that they can turn to the teacher as the authority who will readily help them to structure their learning, and who will act as wise counsellor, impartial judge and sympathetic helper when needed.

Most disciplinary troubles inside the classroom arise because the children either are not interested or have little with which to occupy themselves. 'The Devil finds work for idle hands to do.' Try to develop the ability to take a quick look at the class as a whole, while engaged with a particular group or individual. Adequate preparation of work has a bearing on this, ensuring that you have some idea of how the work might go and that there is enough material to keep every child actively engaged. Most disciplinary troubles will be avoided if there is absorbing, purposeful work for them to do at their own level in an interesting environment. Make sure that a child, having brought a piece of work successfully to a conclusion, has something else to occupy him, such as the continuation of some other work of a different nature, an enjoyable poem, a quiet browse through books in the library corner, some form of art or craft, or is even perhaps allowed a moment or two of quiet reflection.

It may be useful to have a word about noise in the classroom or work area. Children need to be communicative in order to express themselves and to learn. Speech is the best means of communication that a child has; it is the quickest way, and it would be wrong to inhibit his natural desire to contact others through verbal expression. One should expect, therefore, a certain amount of noise from a group of children busily occupied and actively learning. Too much noise, however, can be distracting to certain members of a group, and their needs must also be considered. The teacher's task is to help the children to strike a happy compromise. Anyone whose voice can be heard above the rest is usually making more noise than he ought. Speaking generally, purposeful learning is rarely accompanied by a great deal of chatter or noise.

Children become confused when they are not sure what is expected of them. Be definite with the instructions you give and endeavour to make them as clear as possible and at the child's level of understanding. Children require a certain amount of training in the following of instructions, and constant reminders are necessary. Try to put yourself in the child's place and imagine what he is thinking about the things you say or do (if that is possible). You must remember, however, that too many instructions could frustrate children and discourage some of the spontaneous thought and action which you may very well be trying to develop. A teacher often has to take a course of action which is a compromise in order to maintain a correct balance.

It must not be forgotten that the bearing and personality of the teacher can have a tremendous influence on the class. Wandering about while talking can be disconcerting to those who are listening. Cultivate a voice which carries, is not too high in pitch and has variations in tone; say word endings clearly. Voice and manner are important. A constantly nagging voice can be disturbing and after a while loses its desired effect and creates an unhappy barrier between the source and the recipient. A teacher should be wary of developing, unconsciously, a continually sharp tongue and in fact ought to cultivate a well modulated voice which is pleasant to listen to. It may be necessary that, in order to gain the attention of everyone, you raise your voice slightly, but do lower it when everyone is listening. Set a good example in your speech and expect and insist upon a similar quality from your children.

The voice is not always necessary when the attention of a group is desired. Often a quick look, followed by another in the same direction a few moments later, can command the attention of a wayward pupil about to disturb the concentration of the others while you are telling a story or explaining some point. When a third look fails, a mention of the offending child's name (almost in parenthesis) could be tried; failing this, a position within easy reach of the teacher may be desirable. And failing this, don't give up, thinking that teaching is not for you. Examine what you are saying and how you are saying it. Perhaps you ought to be using an illustration, such as a picture or model, to focus the attention of the class or you may be expecting them to listen for far too long a period without becoming engaged in some activity.

It can be frustrating for a group of children, absorbed in some interesting work, to be constantly distracted by interruptions from the teacher or others present. Therefore avoid interrupting a busy class unless really necessary, and discourage the children from calling out. Rather, allow them to approach you quietly when your assistance is required; and if you are in the habit of circulating among the groups instead of anchoring yourself to a desk, this should be easy for them to do.

Teachers of infant children find that these youngsters often present problems which require subtle handling. There is the awkward situation which can arise because too many children want to do a particularly popular activity at the same time. In this case, alternative suggestion rather than regimentation is the answer; plenty of different activities make things easier, together with a recognized rota which the children readily learn to accept if the reason is explained to them.

Young children enjoy listening to stories but some find it difficult to listen for very long without disturbing those near to them. This can be very distracting for everyone and the wise teacher will ensure that story time is quiet time, even if this means giving a restless child an alternative such as making up a jigsaw or looking at his own book away from the group. In time he feels 'out of things' and is more ready to conform and listen quietly.

It is important that a child learns to finish whatever he has set out to do, whether it is a picture in a book of his own or even a sentence he is copying. But the teacher needs to accept that this is not always possible in the early stages of learning to write, when a great deal of effort and concentration are needed on the part of the child. Praise and the incentive of having a finished piece on the wall will help far more than negative criticism, which is often frustrating to a child who really is doing his best.

When children are new to school, much training is needed in the formation of habits of tidiness. The teacher should insist that the children replace things in an orderly fashion in the cupbords, and if crayons, for instance, drop on the floor, children should be reminded that they need to be picked up. Hats, coats, gym shoes, etc., will soon be lost if not looked after, and a tidy personal locker or drawer is good training for future orderliness. Time and patience are needed for this early training but it is well rewarded. A few children are naturally tidy but the majority just cannot be bothered unless the habit is established in the early days and occasionally revived.

If a young child is particularly aggressive on several occasions and this is obviously more than high spirits, the reasons should be sought. A quiet talk away from the other children about his likes and dislikes and about things at home, may help the teacher to assess the reasons for the child's behaviour. He could be helped to see that it is unkind to hurt others and that he might think differently if the tables were turned. If reasoning fails, a talk with the mother could solve most of the trouble, unless the mother is a primary cause of the child's being anti-social! The causes of some aggressiveness can be very involved and the advice of the head teacher should be sought when real difficulties arise.

Within most schools there are some children who find difficulty in conforming to the pattern of behaviour considered necessary for the correct functioning of the school and for the well-being of each child. One of the hardest tasks with which a teacher is faced is that of helping a child to become part of a group, firstly of a small one, then of the larger one of the whole school, while at the same time maintaining his own identity and personality. Too much individual freedom may lead to selfishness and little consideration for others; but too much conformance to set rules could produce inward rebellion, indifference and passiveness. A good teacher is constantly looking for any of these characteristics and can often anticipate their development and attempt to find remedies. Indifference and apparent laziness could be caused by lack of sleep – it is wise to check on this – or a child could genuinely be bored. Stand back and take an objective look at your classroom and what you are providing for the children and ask yourself whether the environment is stimulating and whether you have presented your material in an interesting way; and ask yourself also if your relationship with the children is a happy one, free from frustrations caused by an over-anxious teacher or a feeling of insecurity rooted in the children's uncertainty about what kind of mood the teacher will be in today!

Aggressiveness in younger children has already been mentioned. With older children too the first step should be an attempt to ascertain the main reasons for such behaviour and to discuss possible approaches to the parents with the head teacher. The older child is more able to respond to reasoning and could be asked to try to put himself in the place of the unfortunate children who are suffering as a result of his aggressiveness. The child could be helped to understand that, because he is stronger and possibly bigger than the others, he ought to be protecting them and showing consideration; he should be setting a good example for younger ones to follow. This approach often works, even though several reminders are necessary. If he is still not dissuaded from his actions, corporal punishment is certainly not the answer. A short period of isolation from the other children might prove beneficial, not only as a reminder that the child must learn to be thoughtful of others if he wishes to be made welcome amongst them, but as a simple protection for the other children. Failing this, a straight talk with the parents of the offending child sometimes solves the matter. If it doesn't, then the head teacher might consider asking for the comments of an educational psychologist.

Some of the statements above could be applied to the child who steals. When there is stealing in the classroom or school it is of the utmost importance to discover the culprit if at all possible. Much valuable teaching time can be lost during investigations, but unless a child realizes that his misdemeanour has been discovered, the chances are that he will steal again. Children may steal because they are deprived, because they are jealous of another's possessions, or simply because they think things should be shared, regardless of ownership. Sometimes a child will steal, not from a particular desire to possess an article, but because he is jealous of another child and wishes to deprive him of what he has. Children have been known to take small articles from a desk and to hide them in someone else's school bag or even in a waste-paper basket or behind a radiator. Guilty children have been known to deny their guilt many times, until they have actually begun to believe in their own innocence.

The writer has found that a child will usually admit to having stolen something when an assurance is given that there will be no punishment, if he is honest, nor will his parents be told – on that occasion.

Stealing is much more difficult to cope with when there are few moral standards set or expected at home. When this is so the school has an even greater responsibility. It must provide an environment where the child can learn to respect the person and property of others and, in turn, expect his companions to behave in the same way. The school, therefore, becomes a place where children learn to live together – an extension of the good home.

Chapter 4

Teaching English

A THE TEACHING OF READING

There is no perfect scheme for teaching a child to read, and it is not intended to propound here the virtues of any particular method. The comparative values of Sentence, Look and Say, Phonic, and Colour Factor methods are dealt with adequately in any course of teacher training, so need not be discussed here. The use of the Initial Teaching Alphabet also receives treatment and the practical details, sufficient to fill a larger book than this, would also be inappropriate here; similarly would the details of the Science Research Associates (S.R.A.) Reading Laboratories methods used in many schools in the USA and now becoming popular in England. It is suggested that, whichever schemes are used, certain practical approaches are common to all, and these will be discussed.

We must remember that the mastery of the mechanics of reading is just a beginning. Once a child can read, vast avenues of exploration are open to him, both in fiction and non-fiction. A child must learn to understand the written word and to write it. Moreover, our task is to guide this learning in such a way that he will have a continuing desire both to read and to express himself in writing.

Outside school, children are continually surrounded by the written word – on T.V. and posters, in comics and books. It is natural, because of children's inquisitive natures, that they will seek to satisfy their desire to know what this or that says. In the classroom, the child should find an environment where written words attract attention. If these words he finds have pleasurable connotations such as birthdays, helpers' lists, collections on the interest table, nursery rhymes, and favourite stories, they will have a greater impact. A child's own name and those of his friends, written on their personal lockers or plimsoll bags, are soon learned. Colourful and attractive books should always be on display for a child to see and touch and from them the teacher can read to the class or group occasionally.

Pictures that the children have brought or have cut from magazines supplied by the teacher, could be pasted into a large book and suitable words written as captions. A child could make his own picture word book including pictures painted or crayoned himself with simple interesting words and phrases described by the child and written by the teacher. The child could firstly follow the shapes of the teacher's letters and words with his finger, then with a crayon, and later copy the words underneath. It is necessary for the teacher to write letters large for children to copy. A thick pencil or crayon for the child is preferable, in order to assist manual dexterity. This kind of activity should create an interest in the written word; show the child that the spoken word has a written form, and help him to associate books with stories. It follows that younger children particularly should constantly be listening to good stories told well. This will further their interest in books and in addition will create imaginative experiences and frames of reference on which future learning can be built.

It is a good plan to have large copies of some pictures which can be found in easy reading books. These could be talked about with small groups of children and labels attached, initially names of children in the pictures, and later phrases and appropriate short sentences. These could be displayed round the room and children given the opportunity to match certain words written on pieces of coloured card with those as captions to the pictures.

When a child readily recognizes and matches the words, this usually indicates that he is ready to be introduced to an easy reading book, preferably containing replicas of the attractive pictures already seen, and words already made familiar.

It must be appreciated that, although a group of children may be considered ready to begin this early stage of learning to read, their rate of progress will vary, sometimes to a large extent. To exert unnecessary pressure at this point could prove disastrous, causing a child to develop a fear of failure and a distaste for reading. It may be advisable to wait for quite a time before some children are ready to continue the process of learning to read beyond a certain stage. Periods of consolidation are often necessary, and the teacher must be patient while at the same time constantly presenting words and pictures and opportunities for oral expression so that, when the time is ripe for further progress, the child is in a position to grasp it.

Learning to read by the recognition of word and sentence shapes alone would limit progress because each complete word would have to be learned as one whole. The subdivision of words into their phonetical structure (the same letter or combination of letters for the same sound) enables a transfer from one word to another, thus allowing the synthesis of new words (word building). As children become proficient in the combination of letters and double letter sounds they are able to use this ability as a tool for expressing their own words on paper.

Word building should have simple beginnings, using a familiar word with two or three letters which is introduced individually as a child is reading to the teacher; for example, a known word split into letter sounds: *b-a-t* or *d-o-g*. In addition to this, a parallel but more systematic approach is to deal with one letter from a known word and to find words which begin with that letter. Later, double letter sounds can be introduced in this way; for example, *ch* and *sh*. It is important to remember that the words chosen should have a link with those in the books that the children are reading or will read in the near future. It has been found from experience that children learn more readily by the use of these methods when working individually or in small groups.

A suggested progression of word building would be:

(a) Choice of the more commonly used words beginning with a particular letter, e.g. *b*ag, *b*oard, *b*asket, *b*oy, *b*all.

(b) Three-letter words with the same vowel sounds in the middle, e.g. b*a*g, p*a*n, t*a*p, c*a*t.

It is a good plan to use games with cards on the floor or table where the child has to pick out a word that matches a word on a master card. When he finds the right card he then writes or traces the letters. Matching cards with words split into two or three parts can help with word building, for example, *sh-o-p*. There are many variations of this.

(c) Double vowels making one sound like *oa* as in b*oa*t and c*oa*t, and *ee* as in s*ee* and sh*ee*p.

(d) Words with similar endings (*-ing* and *-ed* need stressing).

(e) Words having the silent or 'magic' *e* at the end which alters the sound of the other vowels.

The foregoing is but a brief outline.

Books dealing with this topic are usually supplied by the advocates of particular reading schemes, and you would be well advised to study one or two in order to formulate a method of guiding the children which best suits you and the children you teach.

Speaking generally, a good scheme of reading should take into account individual differences and allow for individual levels of reading ability. The more children can help themselves the better, thus relieving the teacher of much laborious record-keeping and repetition.

Most children are anxious to read, particularly when they have been suitably stimulated, and the teacher's task is to try to maintain this enthusiasm. Written expression should not be divorced from reading and, in fact, the two are complementary. Encourage the children to write their own thoughts about pictures and events. Imagine the child's sense of achievement when is is able to insert a word himself into a sentence spoken by him and written by the teacher for him to copy!

When the child is able to write a few words for himself, he needs a word book for easy reference. Small individual books made by folding larger sheets and stapling are very useful for listing words that the child has used and which he will probably need again in the near future. Large class wall books are useful in this context, and could contain helpful words, phrases and pictures about subjects likely to be written about, such as 'The House', 'Clothes', 'Playing', 'The Railway Station', 'Action Words', etc.

The learning of both reading and writing skills will progress side by side and will become complementary. In order to maintain interest a child must not be drilled too much; nor must the teacher use excessive pressure on the child to acquire these skills, if he is to maintain an interest in reading and a love of books. It is inevitable that some children will take much longer than others to master the mechanics of reading. A few will reach junior age before they are able to recognize even simple words or to build them from the letter sounds. If you become responsible for a class or group containing backward readers, it would be advisable to make a careful study of each child's particular difficulties and to use appropriate measures, based on the foregoing, but using a vocabulary commensurate with these children's experiences. Although less advanced with their reading, these children will have been progressing in their experiences of life and will therefore require books more suited to their age and maturity, but having a simple basic vocabulary. Therefore, the teacher's task will be to continue to stimulate interest in ways that appeal to the older child, for example, nature collections correctly labelled, simple classified lists, books containing lists of words concerning topics of interest, class news-sheets, etc.

Reading practice with these older children is better done individually with the teacher, but when the class is large, two or three children could read to each other occasionally for short periods. You will need to plan odd moments during the day to give additional reading practice to some children while others are engaged in activities and assignments requiring less of a teacher's attention. Encourage written expression as this gives a sense of power over words, and also the use of the child's own words and phrases as these are more readily remembered. Children enjoy writing simple stories they have heard.

Before receiving an older class of children who have had some experience of reading, the obvious first step is to ascertain from the previous teacher their reading level and progress. If you wish to assess their reading abilities in comparison with many other children, there are suitable standardized tests available to which you could turn.

For a quick assessment, a word recognition test such as the Schonell or Burt Re-arranged Word Recognition Test could be given, but more comprehensive tests have been developed. The battery of Standard Reading Tests by Daniels and Diack can be used to classify your children, and will help to diagnose individual difficulties. For the first test of Reading Skill you are required to ask a child to read aloud a series of sentences, one being on each page. An advantage of this test over one based on word recognition is that the child is able to use the context and sentence form, thus testing understanding of meaning rather than the pronunciation of words only. The Neale Analysis of Reading Ability and the Holborn Reading Scale also assess and diagnose and can be used with advantage.

Frequent use of tests, however, renders the results less valid, and a period of at least three months between any two testing sessions is usually advisable.

B ENCOURAGING THE YOUNG READER

Some older infants and younger juniors, who have mastered the initial techniques in learning to read, are ready for the transition to library books. These should have simple vocabulary, plenty of illustrations and contain only a few pages. There is a sense of achievement in having read the first library book. It must whet the child's appetite. Try to discover the child's special interests and introduce him to relevant books. All children love a good story and there is a wide field from which to chose. Talk to the child about his book; ask him about the exciting or interesting parts; share it with him. Encourage him to use the class or school library frequently, and at a time you consider appropriate, ask his parents to introduce him to the local library.

Remember also that a child likes to have stories told or read to him. This is your opportunity to share the written word with children. Cultivate the habit of reading aloud with variations in the tone and pitch of your voice. Pause at relevant places to discuss the situation or a character or the development of the plot.

Show children how to make their own books of all shapes and sizes, containing the retelling of stories already heard or read, highlighting the passages which specially appeal to them; accounts of their own experiences, suitably illustrated, and their own imaginative stories, again illustrated, and suitably bound. A collection of these could be made in the class library so that children can read one another's efforts.

Work Cards

Books of information are numerous and most of them are extremely well illustrated. Children require training, however, in searching for information that they can adapt to their own use, for instance in the compiling of information for a folder about, say, 'Our Holidays'. There is a need for the gradual introduction to purposeful searching for information, and a lead should be given. On p. 32 are two illustrations of suitable work cards for a top infant or first year junior class. The use of detailed instructions should help to eliminate the inevitable copying of passages directly from the books being read.

This approach will be developed in the chapter dealing with assignments.

It will be noted that a concrete object which a child can see and feel is given (a cut-out picture could be used as a substitute). Interest is thereby created, then the child is directed to a book that will provide additional information.

Sea-shore Life (stage 1)

(Shell stuck to card)

What kind of shell is this?
Draw one of these shells.
Where could you find one?
How is it attached to the rocks?
Draw some of these shells on rocks.
Find a picture of one of these shells on the table.
What else does the book tell you about the places where this shell can be found and the life of the creature inside?

Sea-shore Life (stage 1)

(Three different kinds of shell stuck to card, e.g. razor, mussel, limpet)

Use a book from the nature table to find the names of these shells.
Write down what you can find out about where each one lives, how it keeps alive, and whether any creatures eat it.
Draw each shell.

The following shows the progression to two further stages. It will be seen that the questions allow for wider reading and require a more mature approach – but this the approach should not be used until adequate experience is given in the earlier stages.

This type of work is developed further in Chapter 6 on Environmental Studies.

Pond Life (stage 2)

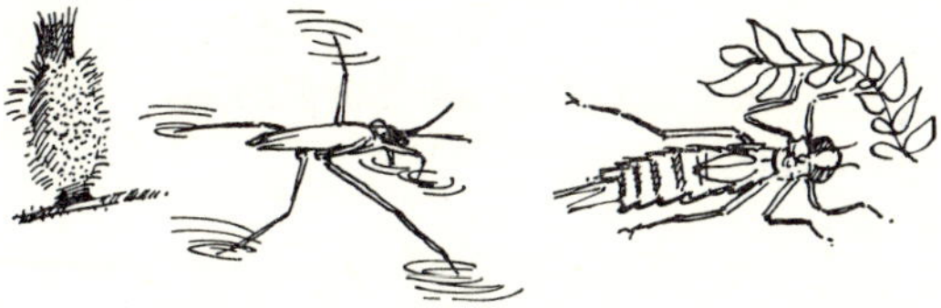

1. Draw these creatures and name them.
2. Use books in the class library to find what you can about:

    Where they live.

    What they eat.

    How they grow.

Here are some questions to help you to start:

What kind of eyes has a whirligig beetle?

How does it use them?

How does a water boatman swim, breathe?

Pretend you are a whirligig beetle.

This is you:

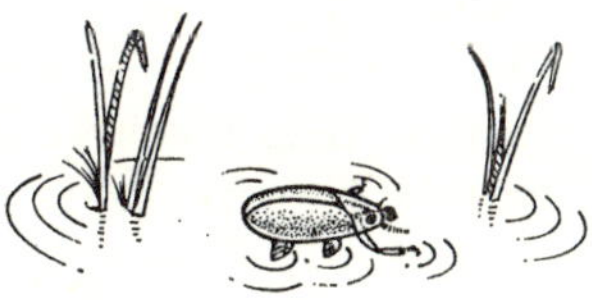

You are in a pond in the country. Write about your day's adventures. Make it exciting.

Begin like this:

I am a whirligig beetle. It is raining on the surface of the pond. . . .

Pond Life (stage 3)

Choose any pond creature or sea creature and write an interesting account of its life. Suggestions:

Life Cycle.

Home.

Food.

Dangers to avoid, camouflage.

Illustrate your account with drawings and cut-out pictures.

Is this creature of any use to man?

C USE AND CARE OF BOOKS

It is advisable always to have books of fiction and non-fiction readily available in class libraries and in the school library. Most schools allow children to take books home, at least from the school library. Plastic sheets offer good protection for books between home and school. Rolls of transparent adhesive plastic can be bought reasonably cheaply and stuck on as a permanent jacket to prolong the life of books belonging to the school. Removable plastic jackets can also be purchased. (See Appendix VI.)

In a class of children there is likely to be quite a wide range of reading abilities and interests. It is therefore important to select library books having a variety of topics and stories and varying in difficulty. If you are in a position to select new books for your class library, here are certain points to bear in mind:

(a) Allow for a wide range of reading ability, e.g. in a class of seven-year-olds the reading age could range from practically nil to ten or eleven.
(b) Beware of lavishly adorned covers with brash colours – the material between does not always justify the exterior. However, most children readily select books that have an attractive meaningful cover.
(c) Read the book yourself, even if only sketchily; read the first chapter in full if you have the time.
(d) With fiction, satisfy yourself that the vocabulary is of good

quality, the characters and incidents are vividly portrayed and the plot is well constructed.

(e) With non-fiction, check that there are clear, accurate and attractive illustrations, the subjects are arranged for easy reference and the information is presented in such a way that children will be stimulated and inspired.

Encyclopaedias have a very useful place in schools, but it is often preferable to have books dealing with individual topics, which are well illustrated and give a wider treatment of the subject.

If you are uncertain about the choice of books, consult such publications as:

Children's Book News – a bi-monthly review of new books chosen by the review panel of the Children's Book Centre Ltd, 140 Kensington Church Street, London, W.8;
Growing Point – issued nine times each year and published by Margery Fisher, Ashton Manor, Northampton;
The School Librarian – the Journal of the School Library Association, Premier House, 150 Southampton Row, London, W.C.1;
The Times Educational Supplement;
Child Education; etc.

Children who have mastered the skill of reading should receive every encouragement to become book-hungry individuals who will have at their disposal plenty of books for their digestion.

Adequate time should be allowed for the children to browse through books in the library, particularly those children who come from homes where there is a dearth of good books. A child needs help in finding his way about the library and in the choice of books for his level of reading ability and understanding. Some children delight in returning to simpler books, read at an earlier age, and they should be allowed to do this occasionally. The teacher's example is invaluable; a love of books is caught more than taught.

Removal of a book from the shelf should be done by placing the forefinger on top of the book, tilting it forwards, then taking hold of the spine with the other fingers and thumb. Pages should be turned over from the top near the outside edge, not from the bottom near the centre. Books should be replaced upright on shelves in the correct order with spines facing outwards, not left lying down on top of other books.

Older children should be taught how to borrow books from and return them to the library, how they are arranged on shelves, how to use the catalogue drawer and the outlines of book classification.

A good teacher will not allow children to use books haphazardly but will ensure that they master certain techniques and skills:

(a) using an index and arranging in alphabetical order;
(b) finding words in a dictionary and searching for meanings of words;
(c) scanning a book to look for particular information;
(d) selecting relevant chapters or passages;
(e) using more than one source to check whether information is correct;
(f) taking the information acquired and presenting it in an attractive and useful form with pictures and diagrams to help with the interpretation;
(g) using encyclopaedias;
(h) using the different parts of a book significantly – contents, illustrations, appendix, bibliography.

Encourage the children to tell one another about the books they have read; discuss books and authors with the children, and give suggestions for suitable reading. This would certainly be valuable experience and could lead to constructive criticism and the writing of book reviews of a simple nature.

Try to improve the quality of books in your classroom by browsing through exhibitions and taking notes on any course you attend, then suggesting titles you would like the head teacher to consider for the next requisition. Attempt to build up a library with a wider scope – single copies of books are preferable to a few sets of the same kind.

D SPEECH AND DRAMA

A conscious effort should be made to improve the speech of your children. This does not mean that the local accent should be frowned upon; rather, it is better to encourage an easy flow of verbal communication and to attempt to improve speech made careless by the omission of words, slurring of sounds, etc. Speech should be clear and lively. One cannot stress too strongly, however, the value of oral work at all levels and in most situations. The spoken word is almost the only means of communication for a young child and it continues to be of prime importance throughout his school life and beyond.

Children need to talk about what they have done, what they would like to do, their likes and dislikes. Encourage them to talk about situations they have experienced, about things brought to school by them and by you, about pictures and books and stories. Creating an interest in books by talking about them is the first step in making a child want to learn to read.

Talking and discussing improve a child's vocabulary tremendously. Many children come from homes which are seriously deprived of books and good vocabulary. It is the task of every teacher to promote the development of this primary means of communication and to make use of it whenever possible. Good speech can be developed through drama and poetry.

Much of the drama developed in schools will spring naturally from stories that have been related, and from situations that have arisen in the classroom or while on an outing – providing that you give encouragement. A box of old materials and clothes should be somewhere within easy reach for dressing up in. Avoid the reading of set plays from books until the children are much older, but allow them to make up their own. The actions and speech may be crude at first. Talk to them about the characters they have chosen to portray and discuss the kind of things such characters would say and do and the sort of clothes they would wear. Point out the necessity for clear speech and meaningful expression, and the need for speaking to the audience, rather than only to one another.

Drama is a natural development of activities associated with physical education and movement. The radio broadcasts for music, movement and mime give ideas that can be developed and applied to a particular class and situation. Help your children to be aware of the space around them and encourage them to use it. Show them how to analyse their movements as heavy or light, strong or weak, high or low, spiked or smooth, etc. and, with older children, progress to other expressive movements using most parts of the body and the face to show pleasure, fear, power, timidity, pleading, etc. Ask the children to demonstrate to one another and to guess what type of action or emotion the other is expressing.

It is helpful when children have been trained in the arts of movement and mime progressively from younger infants upwards. Older juniors then are usually less inhibited and are capable of a wide range of expression.

Music can play an important part in movement and you will find many sources of inspiration in commercially produced records, a selection of which is listed in Appendix VI, or you may like to record snatches of suitable music on a tape recorder. Musical instruments used in schools can provide an excellent source of rhythm and tone drums, tambourines, castanets, triangles, wood blocks, xylophones, glockenspiels, recorders, etc. The drum alone can be very useful, catering for short, sharp or sustained movements, either light or heavy, loud or quiet.

The movement experienced by children can often lead to further expression in art and craft and in descriptive writing; for example:

(1) A middle junior class were engaged in producing different kinds of 'spiky' sharp movements. The teacher led them to think about the possible application of this theme, one group thinking of needles and pins, another of sharp rocks and rock climbing, while a third group thought of witches with pointed nails, pointed hats and sharp features. Mimes soon developed from these themes and the idea of witches encouraged the production of a simple play. In their art and craft the children drew pointed designs and abstract patterns and made models expressing some of the movements they had discovered previously.

Descriptive writing soon followed but it was necessary for the teacher to suggest, through discussion, the possible approaches that could be made. The topics ranged from witches to rock climbing and even included some mathematical vocabulary in the description of angles and pointed geometrical figures. The children made small decorated folders to which they gave such titles as 'My Book of Shapes', 'Angles in Nature', and 'Angular Objects'. Use was also made of the poetry shelves in the class and school libraries, suitable poems being found and read by some children. Several wrote their own poems, on subjects including 'Witches', 'Pointed Things' and 'Lightning'.

(2) Quite often the use of description in stories or poems read to a class of children will suggest dramatic representation and movement. The re-enacting of stories told or read is one of the ways in which a child can associate himself with characters in the story and is a very useful recapitulation of facts and ideas presented.

A class of second-year infants had been listening to the teacher reading the story of 'The Elves and the Shoemaker'. Soon the children were wanting to be the shoemaker, his wife, the elves, etc. It was important to include as many children as possible and in fact the whole of the class had a turn at expressing their ideas to the other children in the room. Discussions followed and suitable key words were written on large sheets of paper in preparation for stories about elves, some of which of course re-told the original story. Pictures were drawn and painted to illustrate the stories and a composite model of the Shoemaker's Workshop was made in a corner of the classroom. Fortunately also, the uncle of one of the children kept a shoe shop and he was persuaded to come into school to talk to the children about how shoes were made. Even mathematics featured in the story when the shoemaker needed to count the pairs of shoes!

These two examples are given with the idea of showing some possibilities, beginning with either a theme or a story. An enterprising teacher will readily find ideas in the many topics of interest, everyday incidents and stories available, to make into an inspired source of learning.

It will be obvious from the foregoing that drama need not and should not be divorced from other aspects of the curriculum. In fact it ought to be an integrated part of a good deal of the work done in the primary school, enabling children to become personally involved, actively rather than passively.

You will notice that some children will stand out as leaders in this field while others are content to stay in the background. You will have some surprises also, because acting brings to the surface talents you hardly expected certain children to possess. Often, those in the background can be persuaded to come forward and take perhaps a small part to begin with, or to be responsible for the scenery, properties, or curtains. Properties and scenery will be demanded, although very little scenery is necessary at this stage, and in the preparation there will be integration with art and craft.

Another method of providing for the shy child is to involve him in the production of a puppet play. The writer recalls how a group of thirty-six eight-year-olds became inolved in a production of 'Rumpelstiltskin' after the teacher had read them the story and some visiting players had performed it to the school. A group of ten children wanted to make the puppet heads, others cut out materials for dresses, some painted scenery and a couple of girls attempted to write an outline of the plot and to divide it into suitable scenes. The most difficult task was the making of the 'theatre' because the children were not content to put two desks a yard apart and to fasten a piece of dark cloth across the front. Eventually a parent who was a joiner was persuaded to knock together a frame around which the children draped curtains. Two boys decided that stage lighting was necessary, so bulb-holders, bulbs, wire and a battery were bought. Their science experiments had taught them about circuits, but in the process of providing lighting for the puppet theatre they invented a circuit with two switches for different coloured lights and discovered the difference between connecting bulbs in series and in parallel. Suitable music was discussed and chosen for appropriate scenes.

Once the play had been performed by a few, others, normally afraid of coming forward and being on view, readily chose a puppet and even entered into meaningful dialogue while they themselves were hidden behind the stage.

Stimulated by all this, the group were able to write very interesting accounts which included character studies, descriptions of how puppets and properties were made and re-tellings of the plot itself, followed by attempts by a few to write their own plays.

E POETRY

Very young children delight in hearing and repeating nursery rhymes and jingles, particularly where there is a chance for actions with fingers, arms and the rest of the body. This is an opportunity not only to enhance clear speech but to develop the vocabulary of number. A teacher's own collection of speech rhymes, poems, etc. which have proved popular and effective with the children, would be invaluable as material to which she could readily turn. Appendix III contains a list of poems the writer has found suitable for various groups. There will obviously be some that are applicable to most children.

Children of any age are usually able to detect a teacher's enthusiasm for poetry, or lack of it. Not all poetry will appeal to an individual, but the chances are that at least one type of poem or certain poets will capture your imagination if you are determined to try. Your efforts will certainly be rewarded by the response of the children with whom you share your enjoyment.

Try to introduce your children to poetry which reflects emotions and experiences they can understand and which, through lively rhythm and forceful diction, appeals to them. The English language has a wealth of simple lyric, narrative and descriptive poetry, so nothing second-rate need be given.

Share poems with your class by reading aloud to them, and allow the children to browse through a plentiful supply of poetry books to discover the poems they prefer. There is little need for young children to 'study' a poem. Reserve that until they have matured enough to be able either to gain greater enjoyment or appreciation by considering metre, form, imagery, diction, etc., or to satisfy perhaps the requirements of certain examinations. Poetry for the children you teach will be primarily something to experience, for a well chosen poem, effectively read, will give its own message.

Avoid using a poem merely as a passage for comprehension. All infants and most junior school children find organized analysis of a poem dull and boring. Do not ask for parts of a poem to be read round the class because it is unfair to the less able readers and to those who have to listen to them, and it may result in little interest being taken except when it becomes that child's turn to read. This applies also to reading prose.

Poems, previously read and carefully selected by the teacher, can be introduced effectively to groups of children or the whole class. Integrate poetry with other subjects and make use of everyday happenings such as the weather – snow, rain, sun – seasons, holidays, adventures, etc.

Most children like to write their own poetry if suitably inspired. Try to eliminate the idea that all poetry must rhyme at the end of each line. Help the children to see that poetry is the choice of good words and phrases to express more clearly what a sensitive person sees or feels. Encourage them by reading poetry and good prose so that they hear the work of experts, then discuss the choice of suitable words to describe a picture, their own actions or a scene which they can experience. At first there will be little distinction between this work and the development of good prose writing. Gradually introduce the rhythm of poetry – again largely through listening to and reading poetry – but keep the accent on meaning and choice of words. It is of little use saying 'Now write a poem about spring' unless the children have been impressed with the beauties of spring, the awakening of nature and the newness of life. A child cannot express the poetry of the local fair unless he has been to see it!

Encourage each child to build up his own anthology of poems, a few suggested by you but more chosen by the individual, suitably written out and illustrated. For a deeper and more long-lasting appreciation, a few poems should be memorized, some in their entirety, others in part. Children may like to say or read their poems to others and some poetry could be used for choral speaking.

F WRITTEN WORK

The foregoing suggestions have been for initial approaches to various aspects of teaching the English language, for both communication and enjoyment. Some of the English you teach, however, will be incidental, for it forms part of almost every learning situation and is an integral part of every subject. Because of this, many teachers find little need for formal instruction in grammar, sentence structure and spelling, a good deal of which can be learned through verbal communication, drama, poetry and the reading of good books. However, a certain amount of direct instruction is necessary with individual children as the need arises or with a group of children whose needs happen to be similar at that particular time. Some learning of grammar will arise naturally from the correction of written work; errors should be corrected with discretion as and when they occur.

Many teachers have found that older children benefit from short exercises in order to correct common faults. These should be used occasionally and when appropriate, not each week as a task to be done from a text book.

Initially there is a need for a child to be able to record statements as simple, sensible sentences having capital letters and full-stops. When a child is ready he should be introduced to the use of a comma for a pause, a question mark when a question is asked and, later, to inverted commas to indicate direct speech. Some teachers prefer to avoid introducing the apostrophe except to the most able children, as this usually results in the decoration of every final 's'. If a youngster speaks correctly he should be aware of the agreement between noun and verb, but in any case, do not underestimate the value of doing a lot of oral work for the improvement of vocabulary, expression and the children's understanding of language and literature.

Older children will need to be aware of parts of speech, the existence of nouns, verbs, adjectives, adverbs and pronouns, but the accent should be on the function of these words, not on exercises which require a child to 'pick out all the nouns and adjectives', etc.

There is need for guidance in the choice and use of words and in the construction of sentences, so that a child may learn to write with increasing variety and precision of meaning. However, instruction in the above must in no way inhibit his ability and desire to express himself readily, with both the spoken and written word. Opportunities should constantly be sought to extend the vocabulary and control of language through the exploitation of everyday experiences, topics of interest and the subjects of the curriculum.

Without 'impression' there can be no effective 'expression'.

Chapter 5

Project and Assignment Work

Successful projects and assignments are not easy to organize but can be extremely rewarding. A good deal of thought and preparation is necessary. It is useless, except with very practised children, to say, for instance, 'Find out what you can about fishing' and to expect a well balanced account with information taken from a variety of sources and presented in an interesting manner. Children need to be trained in progressive stages to gather information, to sift it and to use it well.

Let us imagine that a particular topic has been decided upon, perhaps as a result of discussion with a child or group of children, or from an item of news or interest aroused, or just because it is part of a scheme of work that you are required to follow. How will you further the interests of those concerned with the subject?

If it is a local study a visit might be appropriate. Visits will be discussed in Chapter 6. Various sources of information are available; it will be your responsibility to guide the children to these and to ensure that the best use is made of them. Visual aids such as pictures and wall charts, maps, transparencies, film-strips, movie films and television could be used. Aural aids could include radio broadcasts, tape recordings and records. But the most important source of information is books. These might be found in your class library or local library. The subject chosen will determine the type of source most suitable. Having ascertained where to obtain the information, what is the next step?

We have already intimated that, certainly in the early stages, children require a fair amount of guidance. You will need to suggest to them, by either word of mouth or written assignment cards, where to begin and how possibly to approach the work. Care must be taken here, however, that the children are guided to discover for themselves the wonders of the world, rather than having lists of facts to learn and adult ideas imposed upon them. You will find that throughout your teaching career you will be constantly modifying the ways in which you guide children, in the light of your own experience of how they learn.

Teachers of large classes often find it helpful to write out assignment cards for children to follow, varying the wording and requirements according to the particular child. It is important to remember that it is not in the child's best interests always to be at 'stage one', and the good teacher ensures that there is adequate progression as the child matures. In the early stages it may be necessary to direct a child to a certain picture or chart in one part of the room or to a page in a book. Direction to only a paragraph in one book but a chapter in another may help him to realize the importance of using various sources of information. Later he will have to be taught how to use an index. Then there may be a film-strip or tape recording that will create an interest that could be followed up in a variety of ways. After short periods of instruction, even young children are capable of showing their own film-strips, playing back a tape recording or switching on a record player.

The easiest way for children to find suitable books is for the teacher to gather them from the various sources and place them on a suitable table in the classroom. The next step is for the child to find the required book on the shelves of the class library. Class libraries should have books classified into at least two categories: fiction and non-fiction. If you have enough books for further classification you might like to arrange the non-fiction into general subject groupings, like Geography, Nature, History, Science, etc. Some teachers find it helpful to place small coloured labels on the spines of books, each colour representing a general subject.

Later, children could be taught to search out particular books in a larger central library if you have one in school, or in the local town library. It may be possible, by the way, to borrow small collections of books about particular topics from the local or county library for several weeks at a time.

The guidance you give the child must of course be clear and at his level of understanding. This is why commercially produced cards of instructions are not always effective. A classroom-produced card can be 'tailor made' to suit the individual or group. Many topics are adaptable in such a way that children of various ages and levels of ability can benefit from studying them. Some topics, because of their complexity, are better dealt with by the more advanced and mature children.

If ideas are not given in your schemes of work, you will have the difficult job of deciding which are the most advantageous topics of study for your children, unless you are lucky enough to teach children who themselves provide you with the answer.

Not all information discovered or impressions made need to be recorded. Nevertheless, the habit of recording one's discoveries is a good one and should be developed. Some children might find drama or movement suitable media for showing their discoveries and expressing their impressions; others might prefer to use a tape recorder or take photographs themselves for display on a frieze; some children may find expression in art and craftwork; many will want to produce their own or group folders, written and illustrated. There will often be a combination of two or more of the above.

Discussion with the children beforehand is most important. Not only is it necessary to consider which methods are the most suitable in each case, but also how the children will tackle the job. Lettering, for instance, needs to be practised, and this may well create an interest in the history and types of lettering, which could be a topic of study on its own.

What proportion of writing to illustration will be employed and, in fact, what kind of illustration? In this type of work, it is good to break away from the traditional exercise book and for the children to make their own booklets or folders and to staple or stitch them. The number of pages and the size and shape of the booklets will have to be determined. Each child must be helped to understand that the presentation of such work is important and that a certain amount of pride and satisfaction of achievement can be gained from a task well done. Other people will view and read of his discoveries; therefore only his best is good enough.

When we write an important letter, we first make rough notes, unless we can claim to be very accomplished in this art. Therefore a child will feel the need to jot down notes, sift them and make a rough account for you, as his teacher, to read and comment upon. He may even want his friend or partner to read what he had written and discuss it with him. You will be able to determine the method most suitable to the child. It is better to correct or discuss rough notes for alteration than work intended for final presentation. This will avoid the embarrassment of red-ink marks and repeated corrections. Some children will require much more guidance than others and the very able child might well be able to make his first attempt his last because of the few mistakes he will make. It may be possible for children to discuss their work in groups and even to give short accounts to others in the class. If plenty of interest has been aroused, resulting in a good deal of information and illustration, then this should not be difficult for children to do, even in a limited way.

An incentive to children to present their work well is the provision of a table or, if possible, a corner of the room where work can be displayed. This is where team work can be employed. A few children could be responsible for a background frieze, some others for a composite model, while another group could illustrate through picture and diagram. Most children will wish to have their own booklets on display. When the material to be presented is organized in this way, opportunities are given to the less able child who finds reading and writing difficult but is in his element when drawing or painting. Avoid, however, accepting only drawings and paintings from certain children. Even a poor standard of writing or illustration for display should be accepted provided it is a child's best.

Sample Assignment Cards

The early use of an assignment card was illustrated in the chapter dealing with the use of books. Such cards can, of course, be used to direct children to suitable sources of information and to visual aids such as pictures, maps and films, and even to suggest the making of craft models and different kinds of art work.

The form and layout of the following samples of assignment cards should be self-explanatory and act as a basis for the production of others to suit the particular children and the particular situations in which a teacher may find himself.

Make sure that the printing on the cards is clear and large enough for children to read with ease. It is possible to obtain clear plastic pockets from the usual educational suppliers; they will protect the cards and can be used again when the cards require changing.

Red Indians (stage 1)

Find the book *About Red Indians.* There is a picture of an Indian village on the front.

Look at the picture on page 8 and answer these questions in your folder:

1. What is the man wearing on his head, his body, his feet?
2. What is the lady wearing?
3. Draw the Red Indian and his wife and colour your picture.

Read the page opposite the picture and then answer these questions, writing a sentence for each answer underneath your drawing:

4. What is the name given to a Red Indian wife?
5. Draw a tepee and then write about it.
6. What is a tomahawk? Draw one.

Read the rest of the book, then write a few sentences about Red Indians.

Go to the work table and choose materials for making a tepee (mocassin, canoe) then place your model on the Indian camp.

Red Indians (stage 2)

Find the book *Life of a Red Indian.* Answer the questions in sentences:

1. Read Chapter 1.

   (a) What kind of clothes do they wear?
   What are these clothes made from?
   Describe how White Cloud prepares his skins.

(b) Draw and colour a totem pole. (stage 2—*cont*).
What is it used for?

(c) How is the house made?
What is it made from?

2. Read Chapter 3.

(d) How do they make a fire?
How useful is a fire to them?

(e) What do the children do in their spare time?

3. Take another book from the collection on the table and check that the information is the same.
4. Complete your folder by drawing another picture for the front and writing more information about Red Indians.
You may use any two of the pictures in the box to stick on your folder.
5. Make a model in clay, polystyrene, card, or any material you like, that will show something about Red Indian life.

Red Indians (stage 3)

Make your own folder about Red Indians and choose a title.

Sources of Information:

(a) Books – use catalogue drawer and borrow at least two books from the school or class library.

(b) Film-strips from drawer – use projector and desk screen with your partner.

Use these suggestions as a guide to write an account of Red Indian life, *past* and *present*, with suitable illustrations.

Homes. (stage 3—*cont.*)
Food.
Clothing.
Need for hunting, what they hunt, weapons. Describe a hunting party.
How a Red Indian's life differs from ours.
How they spend their spare time.

Do you think a Red Indian would prefer his present life to that of his grandfather when he was a young man?

Imagine you are a Red Indian boy or girl and write an interesting account of a day in your life.

Tea (older junior children)
(This work would probably last for several weeks.)

1. On your map of the world: (a) Colour the British Isles; (b) Choose another colour and shade all the countries from which tea comes; (c) Draw the route a ship would take from these countries to Britain; (d) Mark and name the British harbour used.
2. Using any books or charts you wish, find as much information as you can and make notes about the following. Later, these notes, together with diagrams and pictures, need to be written (as sentences) in your booklet using these headings:

   Where tea comes from. What it is made of. How it grows.

   The climate necessary. What makes it grow well?
   What part of the plant is used? How are the leaves gathered?
   What happens to the tea before it is shipped to Britain?

(older children—*cont.*)

Mention: the packeting of tea;
costs of different kinds of tea.

3. On a map of Britain show: (a) your own town, London, Edinburgh; (b) the port used by ships bringing tea to us; (c) the route from the port to your own town.
4. Decide the country from which most of our tea comes and find as much information as you can about:
   (a) The climate in summer and winter.
   (b) The high and low land (relief), main towns and ports. Draw a map to show these things.
   (c) What food the people eat.
   (d) What they wear (draw costumes).
   (e) Some of their customs.
   (f) The main exports and imports of that country.
5. What can you discover about the history of the country?
   Is the country in the news at the moment? Why?
6. What can you find out about: the Boston Tea Party? the Mad Hatter's Tea Party?
7. Describe how you would prepare a pot of tea for a meal.
8. Tell why you like tea and find suitable words to describe it.
9. Write a story about a tea plantation.

Chapter 6

Environmental Studies and Local Visits

Environmental studies and educational visits can be of immense value if well organized, but a waste of time if done haphazardly. A successful visit must be preceded by a considerable amount of preparation, firstly with the arrangements for travel, secondly in discussions and preliminary research which prepare the children

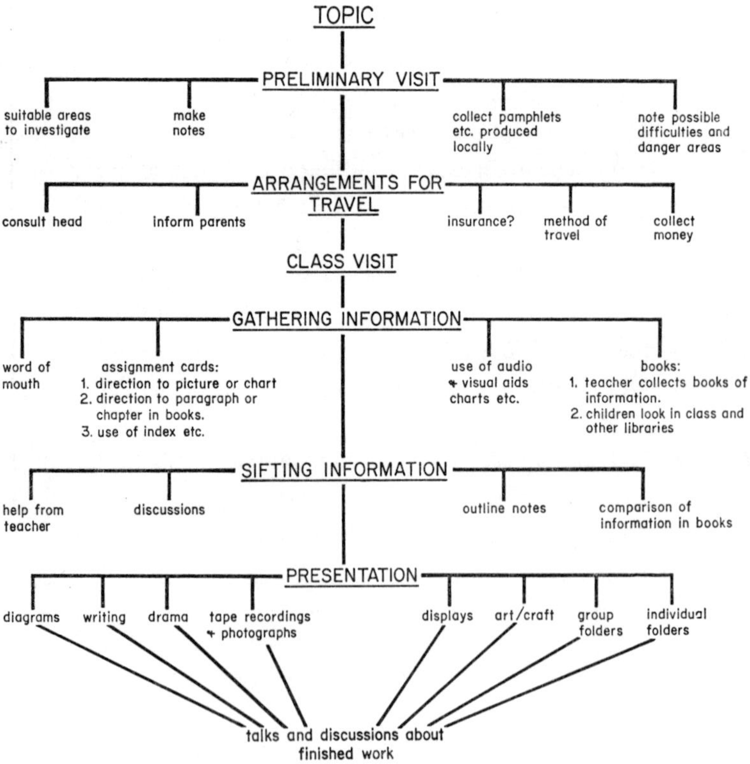

8. Schematic Guide to an Environmental Study.

for efficient and worth-while observation. There must also be adequate follow-up and guidance about the interpretation of the information acquired and its presentation. A guide to activity is presented schematically in diagram 8.

Educational visits can therefore be considered in three phases, (1) preparation, (2) actual visit, and (3) follow-up.

(1) *Preparation*

(a) *Travel arrangements.* Having decided where you wish to go, permission must be sought from the head teacher who will advise on whether you need to inform the parents and whether it is perhaps necessary to obtain their permission. When the expedition is of more than half a day's duration, the Education Authority has usually to be informed.

Many visits require no transport, but when a coach is required it must be booked in good time and the source of money for it determined. Ascertain also for long journeys the amount of insurance cover arranged by the L.E.A. and consider whether it is enough.

(b) *Planning the work.* It is highly recommended that a preliminary visit be made so that any difficulties can be anticipated and details of avenues to explore noted. In fact, adequate and relevant preparation for the visit can only be made when the actual situation has been observed by the teacher.

Having noted the possibilities, the next step is to prepare the children so that they will have an idea of what to look for. Talk to them, point out areas of exploration and give an account of the general background. Almost certainly work sheets will be needed, giving directions or asking questions. Children learn very little when wandering aimlessly about and become very restless.

(2) *Visit*

If you are leaving the immediate neighbourhood of the school at least two teachers are necessary, in case of accidents. An efficient holder for the children's notes is a piece of strawboard slightly larger than the largest sheet of paper, with two clips at the top; small paper clips are not usually large enough, but would suffice if there is nothing else available. Remember also pencils and possibly crayons for sketching, holders and plastic containers for specimens, instruments for measuring, etc.

Some children, on leaving the school premises, immediately feel the freedom of the open air. An early word with these adventurers should curb over-exuberance and help them to understand that, although you wish them to enjoy the visit, you are ultimately responsible for their safety, and the good name of the school is at stake.

(3) *Follow-up*

Perhaps the most important part of projects such as these is the gathering together of the information, specimens and samples, and the recognition, classification and presentation that follow. So many avenues for further investigation and study are often opened up.

Children are keen to have their efforts recognized. They will be ready to display material brought into the classroom and to make records either pictorially or in writing for others to see. The wise teacher will expect high standards of presentation and display and will help to further the children's interests in their recent discoveries by encouraging them to ask questions about what they have found, so that they have a desire to discover more through further investigation and reading.

Of course, the reader will have realized that the follow-up activities are also a very effective means of revision. Displayed facts must be accurate. Diagrams, graphs, drawings on view must be correct, clear and well presented; writing which will be studied by other children and adults must be neat, easy to read and understand, free from simple spelling mistakes, and clearly and concisely written in an interesting manner.

The main difficulty for the teacher to overcome is the co-ordination of this work and the allocation of jobs to each child so that all are purposefully engaged. Do not fall into the trap of thinking that all activity is purposeful. A class or group might readily give the impression, because of the use of much paper and paste, that they are actively learning. Analyse the various activities to ascertain that each one is progressing towards some satisfactory end. Make sure also that certain children do not always do the writing while others, who are good artists, always do the diagrams and paintings. It is good for children to attempt all the various activities, in order to extend their experiences and practise different skills.

For the displays, make use of balsa wood pieces which are easily fastened together with panel pins, boxes made from card, coloured material, and corrugated card for a background.

Some Practical Examples of Work connected with visits and Local Studies

Geographical expedition

Thirty-six boys and girls from a fourth-year junior class became interested in rock formations after one boy had brought a sample of shale for the museum table. Why was it flaky? Why so smooth when wet? These questions and several others were asked and the answers sought from books in the school and class libraries. A discussion ensued, and it was decided that an expedition to the hills about two miles from the school was called for, so preparations were made. Children were to arm themselves with pencils and paper for sketching, a few plastic bags for soil samples, a bucket for suitable pieces of rock, and small trowels.

The teacher, having paid a visit to the area, had seen other possibilities for study so had prepared questions for everyone and had suggested the inclusion of rods marked in inches, measuring-tapes, a stop-watch, etc. Further samples of shale were not available but the children found limestone and sandstone. The limestone was recognized later by the small shells visible under a powerful hand lens. The sandstone crumbled when rubbed hard and this rock was compared with pictures in a book of rocks.

The children found an old quarry and noticed how some rocks occurred in layers and how some looked as if they had sunk below the rest where a crack was visible. Some layers of rock broke the surface and were easily seen. Small samples were collected and placed in plastic bags.

Samples of soil were also taken and these were later subjected to simple analysis: what the soil contained, moisture content, acidity, how much of it burned, etc.

A small stream, the source of which was in the distant hills, led to a discussion on gradients and why the heights of hills and mountains are given as above sea level. The depth of the stream was measured at places about half a mile apart, and the speed of flow was calculated by timing the travel of sticks thrown into the water. An attempt was made to measure the area of the cross-section of the water at a certain point where it passed under a bridge, and a rough estimate of the amount of water passing under the bridge every hour was made.

The samples gathered and information found, together with

accounts of the expedition, were later displayed in the corridor outside the classroom.

Local study – elections

Interest in the Borough Elections initiated a series of studies related to the locality for eleven-year-old children of mixed abilities.

Discussions concerning the function of the local Council were held and the children were taken to hear and see an open session of the Council. This led to a consideration of the amenities of the town and of what should be provided to make it a more desirable place in which to live and work. This is what one boy wrote:

> 'I think there should be a subway underneath the busy main road which passes through the town. This would reduce accidents and prevent waiting for both pedestrians and traffic.
>
> 'Play streets should be provided in some parts of the town. You would appreciate this because, besides being fewer accidents, children would not be interrupted in their games.
>
> 'A zoo should be made in part of the park so that children and adults could see all kinds of animals.
>
> 'There should also be more facilities for those wishing to take part in sports.'

Several children asked if they could organize their own mock election in the classroom. Some election pamphlets were obtained but the children candidates preferred to have their own ideas about the government of the town and the amenities required. Election speeches were drafted and four candidates each attempted to persuade others that their ideas were the most beneficial for the town. Party politics were of course avoided. One child was duly elected and majorities and percentage votes were declared.

The children were reminded that the improvements suggested would cost money. The reason for the levy of a rate was explained and several children who lived in the Borough and the outlying Rural Districts brought their fathers' Rate Demand Notes. The items on the back were discussed and a lesson on the fractional parts of a pound allocated to the various amenities, proved very informative and realistic. The children were surprised to find how much of the money was allocated to their education!

One of the items was for the upkeep of the Police Force, and as three of them were policemen's children, it was decided that use be made of this contact. A constable was invited to the school and he talked to the children about his job and explained the various duties a policeman has. They were very interested in his transmitting and receiving set, particularly when he allowed them to listen to calls being received from Headquarters.

The Town Hall proved to be helpful for quite an unexpected reason. While studying a map of the town, one group expressed a wish that they could actually see the town from above, and the Town Hall was suggested as a suitable high point. From the top

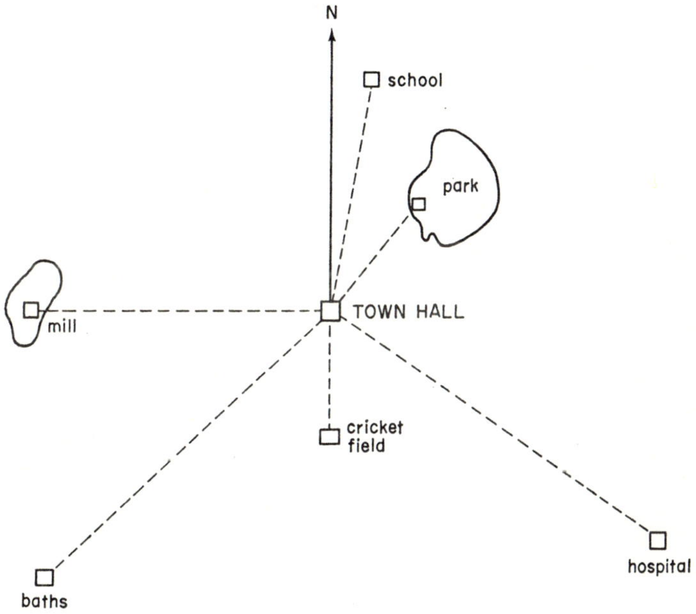

9. Plotting Positions.

observation windows there was a panoramic view of the town and surrounding districts and, as the teacher had anticipated, the children were soon requesting another visit so that maps seen in the school could be compared with the actual terrain. Maps of scales $2\frac{1}{2}$ in. and 6 in. to the mile were used. First the maps were orientated (N. on the map pointing to north). One boy pointed out that the compass was really pointing to magnetic north and a small correction had to be made. Reasons for this were discussed later at school.

The teacher had (by chance!) brought along two clinometers, one of which had been made by a previous class. Soon the children were taking readings of various landmarks to find the declination from the observation window, the height of which was determined by taking a reading of its angle of elevation from the ground before returning to school. Using the small compasses and an observer's compass for greater accuracy, children were able to determine the direction from the Town Hall of the various landmarks referred to above.

Back at school, scale drawings were made, using the angles measured from the observation window, and the distances and directions of the various places were checked against the maps. It was thus possible to build up a simple map of the area using the Town Hall as a focal point (diagram 9).

From such an elevated position it was possible to put things more into perspective; to see one's school, one's home, in relation to other things; to realize that the town was a living, vital community.

The information obtained and calculations made, were illustrated and described and then displayed along a corridor in school for all to see.

Local historical visit

Another class, this time of nine- and ten-year-olds, decided to find out whether there had been any outstanding people who had lived locally. They discussed how they could find such information and a list of possible places was made. One was an old hall in the park and the other a much older building which could possibly contain records – the parish church.

A preliminary visit by the teacher made possible an outline of work which was presented as suggestions on work cards given to small groups of children. Here is a selection of the questions used:

Find the sundial and sketch it; how can it be used?
Sketch the tower and find its age.
What do we call the queer faces carved in stone which are at roof height? What is their use?
Of what kind of stone is the church made? Sketch the part you like best.
Why is the Patron Saint St Laurence?

Find the grave which has been in the churchyard the longest time. Make a rubbing of the lettering.

Draw the shields on the gate. What do the different parts stand for? (This led later to an interest in heraldry.)

Find the Standish pew. Who was Miles Standish? (This led to much interest in the Pilgrim Fathers.)

Look at the stained-glass windows. What do they show? Make a note of the figures shown in them and what they are doing. Find out more about the people.

The children set about their tasks immediately. Three-quarters of an hour later the class of thirty-six children was split into two groups and each toured the church as a party. The curate and verger were present and they answered children's questions. The verger showed the children the church plate (which later led to an interest in silver and why it was valuable) and the curate let the group see a parish register 500 years old. They were very surprised to see such ornate writing, and the styles of the various entries over the years were compared with each other and with the children's own writing. Copies were made for display at school. Rubbings of gravestone lettering added to the display, a simple selection of various letters being arranged in an attempt to show the development in style. This could have led to a project on the general development of styles of lettering but somehow the interest was lost. This was a pity because books were available. Perhaps the idea will be revived at a later date.

The curate told the group that the church had originally been much smaller and that the two passages, one an each side of the main body of the church, had been added in the year 1860. Why was this? There had been more demand for accommodation because of an increase in population. Why was there such an increase? Industrial expansion. There was much food for thought here. It so happened that the teacher had obtained from the County Archivist maps showing the town in 1768, 1845, 1894, and 1930, together with old documents such as letters, bills, requests, etc. Population graphs were drawn and the children were able to see at first hand the changing pattern of society.

A special loan of books was obtained from the county branch library and several children became involved in interesting stories of the Industrial Revolution. The teacher made cards with relevant questions directing the children either to particular pages or to sections of books in order to help them glean information about the Pilgrim Fathers, the Civil War and the Industrial Revolution. They learned how people travelled in those days, how they dressed, lived and worked, and what they ate. A film about the Pilgrim Fathers was obtained.

The final effort was a simple but effective service for morning worship, produced by the children, which included short stories about St Laurence and Miles Standish.

Development from a sewing lesson

A class of middle junior girls began asking questions about the materials they were using when sewing and knitting. A discussion with the teacher followed and it was decided to find out more about cotton and wool and how they were produced. The teacher hastily compiled a few work cards directing the children to certain books known to be kept in the class library and central school library. An immediate approach was made to the county library also, asking for a loan of books concerned with cotton, wool and synthetic fibres – the latter being an addition by the teacher in anticipation of further developments.

Some of the children wrote to firms to ask for information and possible samples. These addresses were obtained from a Textile Year Book. The class was given a lesson on business-letter writing, and the children were quite surprised at the difference between an informal and a formal letter. Soon replies were received, containing information (which in some cases was a little difficult for them to interpret), samples of materials and even a shuttle used in cotton weaving. All these were put on display, using three tables against a wall of the classroom with display boards behind.

An approach was made to a local cotton mill asking if they would allow a party of children to see the spinning and weaving carried out there. The reply was favourable, and the children later spent a very informative afternoon asking questions (previously prepared after class discussions) and seeing for themselves the various processes from bale to finished cloth.

In order to help the children to recall what they had seen a filmstrip was shown, and it was not long before very interesting and attractive booklets of information were being produced.

Some of the children expressed a desire to learn how to weave, so simple looms were set up with the idea of producing woollen scarves.

The books dealing with synthetic fibres were displayed on a table and it was not long before the children were anxious to learn more about the garments that many of them wore and which were becoming more popular in the shops. They wrote to several other firms, which supplied more information and samples to be included in booklets and the classroom displays.

By this time – after about four weeks – the interests of some children had begun to wane. The teacher was aware of this, so the whole project was brought to a conclusion. Or was it? The history of cotton spinning that some children had been reading about made them ask questions about the Industrial Revolution!

Discoveries in the park

The school held a bulb show, and the local Park Superintendent came to judge the exhibits. He invited the children to visit his park and as a result a class of eight-year-old children found many interesting things.

Several visits to the park became necessary. The following is a summary of their activities.

A plan of the park was made. Distances were calculated by paces and trundle wheel. The hall, ponds, bowling green, tennis courts, paths and fields were marked. Much more was added later. The children were not of an age to appreciate much about scale, but they readily converted actual measurements once the teacher had suggested a suitable one. An attempt was made to name all the trees and mark them on the map, but the children soon realized the enormity of the task and settled for trees lining, or close to, the paths and pond. Books for tree recognition were obtained from the school and class libraries.

Some children were shown a herbaceous border and it was not long before the names of several plants were known. Further names were discovered in a book on garden flowers and plants. The Park Superintendent told the children about the kind of plants he would choose for the border and the way in which he ensured variety for most of the year.

There were several rockeries in the park which proved very interesting, particularly because the children were able to copy the ideas and make a rockery of their own at school. They learned why certain rocks are suitable and others not, the necessity for arranging them in a certain way, and how the plants help to keep them in place during severe weather. The children had previously taken for granted the large areas of grass around them in the park. They were surprised to hear about the care needed in the selection of seeds, preparation of ground, fertilization and cutting of the grass. Collections of different grasses were made and the children later brought samples from different parts of the countryside and their own gardens and made an attempt to identify them. The display of grasses was very decorative and impressive. (An older class became so interested in the grasses collected by the younger children that they experimented with the growing of different grasses and noted the effects of varying amounts of water and fertilizer.)

It was found necessary to make a second and yet a third visit to the park because there was so much to see and discover. The following are some of the further lines of investigation followed:

Identification of the bulbs grown, planting and growing techniques, costs, parts of bulbs and their functions.
How the worm helps the gardener; life and habits of the worm.
Bees, and how they help to propagate flowers.
Study of other common garden insects.
Birds in the park, identification, how and where they build their nests, how they feed.
Study of the rookery near the parish church.
Fish and plants in the lake and ponds in the park.

FURTHER IDEAS FOR ENVIRONMENTAL STUDIES

Nature collections

Wild flowers. Found in certain places such as ditches, woods, hedges, etc.; pressing between paper and mounting, naming, some sketching and painting, study of parts.
Fruits and seeds. Naming and drawing, painting possibly, study on how they are scattered, e.g. by wind, birds, animals, water.
Colours and patterns. Of feathers, shells, leaves, bark rubbings, twigs, stones, etc.
Tracks made by animals. Plaster casts, identification – could lead to seeking more information about the creatures' habits, etc.
Leaves. Identification and display, leaf prints, patterns with leaves, preservation.

Walks and explorations

Map the route beforehand with simple directions and outstanding points to look for, e.g. churches, stiles, crossroads, bridge; give duplicate maps to pairs of children; provide lists of things to collect and questions to answer about them. It is not always advisable or in fact possible to collect all that is of interest, so questions, some of a general and others of a more precise nature, could be set, the former giving scope for more personal discovery and the latter giving a lead in order to prevent aimless wandering.

Quiz game

Have several interesting items on display for a few days and inform the children that there will be a quiz about them later. Then remove the items before having the quiz.

Water study

Sources of water – try to visit the source of a small river or stream.
What water carries with it downstream.
How a river changes the shape of the countryside.
Water supply to our taps.
Value of water in our diet, in industry.
Minerals in water.
Ponds, pond life.
Properties of water – finding its own level, etc.
Water used for power.
Reservoirs, rainwater.

Weather station

Rain. A gauge can be simply a jam jar with a funnel to prevent evaporation. Pour the rainwater into test tubes or medicine bottles arranged in a row, mark the levels, then draw a graph in the form of a histogram.

Wind. Make a simple anemometer from jelly moulds. Count the number of revolutions per minute. Write out the Beaufort Scale and compare it with the above measurements. Discuss what causes wind to blow. Make a weather vane and mount it high enough to avoid the effect of buildings. Note the compass direction of the wind for at least a week.

Sun. Measure the length of shadows using a vertical stick. Mark the length and direction of the shadows each hour. Record the hours of sunshine.

Temperature. Take the temperature outside in the shade each day, once at a certain time in the morning and again in the afternoon, say at 10 a.m. and 3 p.m. Record this and plot a graph. Repeat for at least a week. Find the average morning and afternoon temperatures. Using a maximum and minimum thermometer note the hottest and coldest part of each twenty-four hours.

Cloud. Discuss cloud formations, their types and how they form. Note the amount of cloud in the sky each day at certain periods, in tenths of the sky covered.

Air pressure and humidity. With older children usually. Study the effect of height, and pressure areas. Measure the moisture in the air outside and in the kitchen.

See also the mathematical suggestions on page 75.

FOLLOW-UP ACTIVITIES

The reader will appreciate that the activities resulting from the foregoing environmental studies may open up many and varied opportunities for further work, and that the presentation of the information discovered, in the form of accounts and displays, constitutes a very effective means of revision. Insist that the information is accurate; that diagrams, graphs and drawings on view are correct, clear and well presented; and that writing which will be studied by others is neat, easy to read and understand, has no simple spelling mistakes, and is written clearly and concisely in an interesting manner.

The teacher's main difficulty is the co-ordination of this work and the allocation of jobs so that all the children are purposefully engaged. Once again let us emphasize the importance of not falling into the trap of thinking that all activity is purposeful. Analyse the various activities to ascertain that each activity is progressing towards some satisfactory end.

Chapter 7

Mathematics

A good teacher will always bear in mind that, as far as possible, children should be motivated in such a way that they want to learn because they are interested in what they are doing. This is particularly true in the field of mathematics. Further, if these children at the same time are actively engaged and suitably guided to discover mathematical concepts and ideas for themselves, they will learn more efficiently and benefit from the development of correct attitudes towards mathematics.

It is because of this that a teacher should aim at giving the children a stimulating environment offering scope for mathematical discoveries. Use should be made of the local situation to make children aware of the mathematics around them. Mathematics should not stand in isolation – there should be an attempt to link it with other subjects and topics so that it becomes an integral part of everyday life.

The methods of helping children to learn this subject in our primary schools vary greatly. On the one hand there is the strict adherence to a text book containing mechanical sums and a few problems often unrelated to a child's immediate experience; while on the other there is the complete abandonment of text books, with the development of mathematical ideas through children's interests. There is the insistence that all the children in a particular class should complete and obtain the correct answers to a fixed number of the same sums, the procedure being repeated each day; and there is the situation where children work either in small groups or individually, each progressing at his own pace.

The use of one particular text book presupposes that there is only one path the learner should take towards the understanding of mathematical concepts and processes, and that all learners require the same amount of practice. On the other hand, many teachers would be distressed to be deprived of the help of a text book, expertly constructed, from which they could draw ideas and suitable samples to present to children. The solution would appear to be to benefit from not only one, but several, books; to have assignment cards suggesting areas of study to follow, which could lead to personal investigations and discoveries; and to work from centres of interest linked to the environment and to selected topics. A teacher will find a host of ideas for this approach in the Nuffield Mathematics books, which give examples of ideas actually tried in schools.

Ten or twenty sums each day for all the class to attempt, from either the blackboard or common text book, is certainly very easy on the teacher, but has the obvious pitfalls of time-waste for the brighter children and confusion and frustration for the less able. Individual working can have the disadvantages of insufficient group support and encouragement, which are required by some children; the possibility of the lazy child's being overlooked; and the difficulty the teacher has to ensure that all children are progressing as they should and that work is marked. Some teachers express with concern that they prefer not to have to explain a method 'forty times' when once or twice would do.

Nevertheless, these difficulties can be resolved by a little thought, effort and practice. Centres of interest and combined efforts for groups of children with everyone making his personal contribution, should help to solve any possible lack of community feeling. When children are working individually there will be as many different rates of progress as there are children. It is essential therefore that adequate records are kept, although it must be remembered that not everyone will necessarily pass through the same stages of understanding in the same order or attain any particular level by travelling a similar route. Your school schemes of work should help here. There will certainly be some duplication of work, but, as we have already discussed, children's learning varies so much that individual tuition as far as possible is, in the long run, more efficient.

Many teachers prefer to organize their classes into groups with the children working sometimes in pairs and quite often individually. This is because: (a) individual needs vary so much that if we expected every child to do the same sum, for instance, it could, as we have previously intimated, be too easy for the bright child who would really be wasting his time, and too difficult perhaps for the dull child who would soon develop a distaste for the mathematics he could not do; and (b) when children work in groups the teacher's time can be spent more economically, because some can be given work which at that moment requires little of the teacher's attention, while others can be introduced to a new step or a particular kind of practical work which may demand a good deal of the teacher's help. By this means the endless queue or sea of upraised hands demanding attention can be minimized.

Another way to reduce the constant demand for the teacher is to allow the children to mark much of their own work, if in fact all of it does require marking! Purely mechanical sums and answers to many other aspects of arithmetic can, and should, be marked by the child himself. Answer books or cards of answers could be placed in selected positions in the classroom or work area with a pencil close by. Some teachers are afraid of allowing this kind of freedom and point out that there would be widespread cheating. This will not occur when there is a happy relationship between teacher and child, when there is not the element of undue competition present, and when the children have been helped to understand that if they call something right that is wrong they are really cheating themselves.

Remember also that although it is important to be able to obtain the right answer, the technique of mastering the elements of a sum or problem and the organization of these techniques progressively towards the right answer are more important than the answer itself, as far as the learning process is concerned. But there is little doubt that children like to see pages with ticks on them – lots of ticks – and they derive great satisfaction from having achieved correct answers. It is essential that children are guided through progressive stages in mathematical understanding and that, as far as possible, concepts and methods are understood before the practice of a skill is attempted.

In an effort to achieve this a good number of schools use structural apparatus. For many years, of course, children have been helped by the use of counters and other objects, including the fingers (and why not, there are very conveniently ten of them if you count thumbs!). The use of apparatus is invaluable as an aid to understanding. There is also the point, however, that mathematics is essentially abstract, so children should be encouraged as soon as possible to discard these aids when there is no longer any need for them. There should be no hard and fast rule here because a child may wish to return to apparatus occasionally in order to verify a calculation and to be confident of the result obtained. It is important that the teacher be continually on the look-out for those children who are failing to see the mathematical ideas, and who are becoming only expert manipulators of apparatus.

A ORGANIZING THE CLASS OR GROUP

If the children you receive are used to more formal lessons, the best advice would be for you to approach informality gradually. Prepare assignment cards and allow a group at a time to tackle the discovery work. If others are busy with text-book arithmetic, this will give you more time to deal with the activity group. You may find initially that you are short of assignment cards and apparatus so a small group would be the best to manage.

After a little while additional time could be given to assignments each week; there may come a time when all the class will be engaged on activity mathematics and the necessary mechanical computations to be learnt will arise from the activities. However, in order for this situation to arise, the teacher will have the difficult task of devising activities that are suitable for the different levels of understanding, and that offer a reasonable progression in the development of mathematical experience. Here again, the school's scheme of work should be a guide. If the children you inherit are used to the above, your task will be much simpler. If not, 'slow but sure' is the answer.

A word of warning. Do not fall into the trap of thinking that because it's on an assignment card it will lead to active learning. Some cards have been known to be copies of an out-of-date text book and a badly written card can involve children in occupations that lead to little or no learning.

The vocabulary of number is very importaant and children should be introduced to the language of mathematics right from the start. At an early age a child can learn to talk about and compare objects that are 'large' or 'small', 'wide' or 'narrow', 'long' or 'short', etc. As he progresses with his knowledge of mathematics, it is essential that terms and vocabulary relative to that level of knowledge be learned so that a fuller understanding can be achieved, the child then being in a position to communicate, understand and be understood more readily.

An adequate command of mathematical vocabulary is necessary for meaningful recording of work. Early recording is done using counters, bricks, stones, pebbles, shells, beads on a string, piles of cotton reels in the shape of a three-dimensional graph, drawn shapes, etc., all of which help to prepare the way for numerical symbols.

A teacher will need to talk about discoveries and processes with children and to discuss interpretation of results, graph work, use of diagrams, etc. Children should be shown how to record in several ways. This will help them to have a better understanding of the problem posed and the ways to achieve an answer. This wider, more varied experience of an approach to the solution (of a problem, experiment, or mechanical computation) puts the learner in the position of being able to use more readily the individual elements by transferring them to other problem situations. This perhaps is the answer to those who would teach a child only one way to do a particular sum, adding the comment that there is 'no time' to deviate from a set path or that 'children will become confused'. Confusion arises when the learner has become 'set', with a particular form of approach, instead of having the confidence and ability to be more flexible. One test by which your success might be measured is to observe the children's reactions to new situations: do they tackle them with enthusiasm based on their previous experiences or do they immediately plead inadequacy because they 'haven't done any of that sort before'?

Some teachers prefer all the children in a particular class to be occupied at the same time with some kind of mathematics. Others, perhaps more adventurous, like to have varied activities in progress at most periods throughout the day.

A successful way of organizing the former would be to arrange the class into several groups containing four, six, or eight children, each group being allotted a particular type of mathematics for that day, e.g.:

Group 1. *Maths Guide Cards* – using blocks or other similar apparatus.

Group 2. *Text Books* – each child working at his own level, not all necessarily using the same type of book.

Group 3. *Group Topic* – preparation of work for a group folder on, say, traffic survey, or follow-up of T.V. broadcast.

Group 4. *Maths Work Cards* – experiments and use of general apparatus to include experience in money, length, weight, time and capacity.

Group 5. *Shop* or *Post Office* for younger children; personal choice or further text book work for older ones.

Each group then changes to another activity the next day, and so on until by the end of the week every child has had a turn at each activity. This arrangement allows the teacher more time to deal with groups that require additional attention, or to introduce a new topic or stage to a group. Apparatus and text books need not be greatly duplicated, but a few of several types can be bought, giving much more variety.

For junior children, when the classroom situation is such that several varied activities are taking place throughout the day, a modified group work based on the foregoing could be employed. The instructions are written on the blackboard or a large direction card. It is important to bear in mind that the levels of difficulty of the various activities should, as far as possible, be equal; otherwise, some of the activities will tend merely to occupy rather than stimulate.

For example:

Today's Programme

Spend some time during the day on all these activities.
Choose in any order you wish.

1. Mathematics.
2. Practise handwriting slopes.
3. Finish writing and drawing for fishing topic.
4. Scripture story.
5. Answer one nature study card.
6. Add to frieze or model ships.
7. Spend about $\frac{1}{4}$ hour on reading practice book and read two pages to me (the teacher) or read library book.

Allow twenty minutes for T.V. at 2.00 p.m. and discussion afterwards.
P.E. 11 to 11.30 a.m.
Maths
A and B Groups – At least one page from maths book, then post office.
C and D Groups – Do a practical card, then project on (say) body measurements.

As well as T.V. and P.E. there would be other class or large group activities, e.g. singing, drama, story, music and radio.

B PREPARING WORK FOR CHILDREN TO DO

Guide Cards for Structural Apparatus

Dienes, Cuisenaire, Color-factor, Stern and other structural materials have their own books or work cards which are available for purchase. Whichever of these materials are available for you to use, try to obtain the teacher's manual and, if possible, a sample of children's books or cards. The least a teacher can do is to read the manual and use the cards provided. But an enterprising teacher will find ways of adapting the commercially produced work cards and selecting certain pages of children's books so that they are more suitable for individual children. For instance, a bright child may not need to complete all examples, while a less able child may require further practice. This ability to adapt material effectively will come with experience. Meanwhile, map out a course of progressive work that you consider is necessary, and change it later.

Text Books

A similar approach should be applied to the use of text books. Some schools prefer a 'basic' or 'anchor' book through which most children progress. This kind of book must be chosen very carefully; no doubt the head teacher will have done just that. Much mechanical computation is not advisable in such a book; rather it should contain ideas for investigation and present a carefully selected programme of mathematical ideas which will help towards an understanding of relationships and processes. If several kinds of text books are available, the teacher should make a note of the parts which are considered to be the most effective and which will provide a useful addition to the work in the 'anchor' book used. It is obvious from the foregoing that a detailed study of text books is essential if the organization is to be done well. If possible, work through the books quickly, attempting some of the examples the children will be doing, and try to anticipate the difficulties which may arise.

Group Topics

Often there will be a contrived situation for study, e.g. the classroom animal's weight, length, food consumption, growth, etc. Mathematics of a class weather station follows later in this chapter.

Sometimes the topic will be related to geography, history or another subject, e.g. after a holiday – collection of postcards, distances to places and times of travel, cost of stamps; clay modelling – shrinkage and loss of water; school meals – graphs of favourite foods, amount of waste each day, proportion wasted; history of number and measurement; model of a house with furnishings to scale.

Maths Work Cards

Cards of various colours are the most suitable, with a different colour for money, length, weight, time, capacity, number, shape, and so on. The work indicated on the cards should show a gradual progression and whenever possible be related to real situations. For example, one teacher asked some infants to measure the lengths of different pieces of wool. The children soon lost interest, but when length of shoes, spans and heights of children were suggested, the response was enthusiastic. Sample cards:

Length (early stage)

You need a ruler and pencil.
How long do you think your shoe is?
Use your ruler to find the length of your shoe.
Write this down:
My shoe is . . . cm long.
Find the length of your friend's shoe.
How much longer or shorter than yours is it?
Write:
My friend's shoe is . . . cm longer (or shorter) than mine.

Length (more difficult)

What are the dimensions of the guinea-pig hutch?
How much air is there inside it?
What length of wood 10 cm wide would be needed to make another hutch?
Find the cost at 10p per metre.

Weight (early stage)

You need the three tins coloured yellow, blue and red.
Which is the heaviest?
Which is the lightest?
(N.B. The heaviest not being the largest)

Weight (more difficult)

Here are some peas.
How many peas would there be in 1 kg?

Here is a sample of a work card made at the time of the Olympic Games:

Olympic Graphs

1. *Make a graph* to show the heights of important places compared with Mexico City 7,400 ft above sea level.
2. Use your atlas to find how high the following places are and include them in your graph:
   Rivington Pike (local landmark).
   Mount Olympus.
   Mount Everest.
   Vesuvius.
   Addis Ababa.

Add any other high places to your graph.
Decide what unit you will use to plan your graph.

C OTHER IDEAS FOR MATHEMATICS TOPICS

Personal measurements (cubit, stature)
Measure your own span, wrist, neck, waist, chest.
How many spans will go round your waist, chest, etc.?

Measure length of desk and room using cubits, span.
How many paces for length of corridor, yard?
How long is your pace? Calculuate length of corridor, yard, etc.
Measure above accurately.
Draw round your foot, and find the area in square cms.
Ask your friend to draw round your body on the floor – what is your area?
Chest expansion.
Speed of your walking, running.

Other measurement and graph work

Times of going to bed.
Heights.
Pets owned.
Sizes of shoes.
Birthdays – months.
Weights.
Length of feet.
Christian names.
Number in family.
Temperatures during day.
Rainfall.
Children's ages relating to height and weight.
Height in relation to weight.
Colour of eyes.
Crisps or biscuits sold.
Favourite author.
Football scores.
Favourite T.V. programmes.
Popular school meals.
Waste each day after school meals.
A Graph Book could be made, in addition to the completion of large wall-display graphs.

Shop or post office

Ask the children to bring empty boxes and cartons which can then be marked with the appropriate prices. For a post office, stamps can be designed and made using potato printing, postal orders can be copied from a sample real one, and telegram forms will be available from the local Post Office.

Work cards are again useful here. They can tell children that they have so much to spend and suggest that they go shopping for several items, for which they will require a bill – one worked out by the shopper and one by the shopkeeper (thus making a useful check on arithmetic).

Sample of a topic using the mathematics of a weather station
Rainfall. Gather in jam jar; pour each day's rain into a test tube; arrange in order.

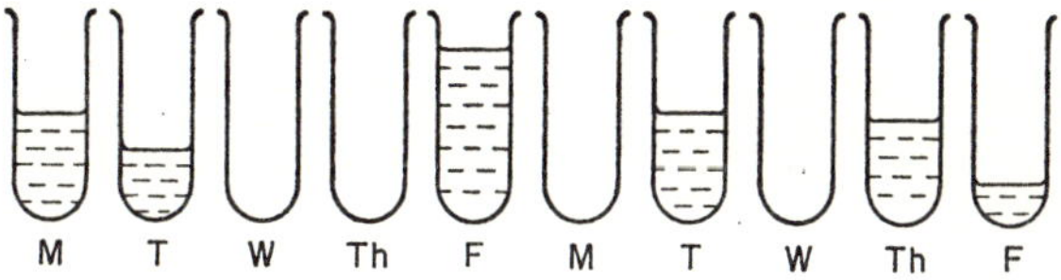

Beginnings of graphwork. Later, a more sophisticated rain gauge could be used and amounts shown on actual graph. Collect rainfall data of local area, county and country averages. Link with geography – rainfall areas of the world and how climate affects life, products, etc.
Wind. Speed – make a simple anemometer from jelly moulds; count number of revolutions in a minute. Compare with Beaufort Scale. Direction of wind – make a weather vane; compass points. Relation to maps – further study.
Sun. Amount of sunshine – further graph work. Length of shadow using a shadow stick – shows variation of sun's height in sky.
Temperature. Introduction to thermometer. Scale (usually 1:2). Link with science – expansion. Addition and subtraction practice, e.g. 21 degrees to 45 degrees, increase?; also decrease and idea of negative numbers, e.g. below zero. Temperatures in shade; also maximum and minimum, coldest and warmest part of each twenty-four hours – graph. Country and world temperatures. Link with rainfall investigations.
Air pressure. Older children can make and use a simple barometer. Isobars. Changes in pressure related to weather. Introduction to weather maps and tape recording of weather forecasts for land and shipping. Link with geography.

This work can involve not just one class but all the school. Children of different ages and levels of ability are thus able to contribute to the development of a weather station.

D INTRODUCING BASIC UNITS

Money

The understanding of number should develop side by side with the use of decimal currency, the learning of the one reinforcing that of the other. Let children handle coins or tokens and practise shopping so that they become aware of the procedures necessary. For example, they will need to recognize the coins in relation to one another so that change can be given and calculations of addition and substraction made.

Encourage children to use the largest value coin possible when shopping or calculating and stress the relationships of the numbers ten, five and two. For instance, weekly dinner money amounting to 49p would be given as 4 tens +5p+2p+2p, or as 50p with change 1p.

Stress counting in tens and later in ten tens to make a hundred, which is of course the number of pence in £1. It will be seen from the foregoing that a sound knowledge of the number system is important and an early introduction to decimal notation will be necessary in order to appreciate the meaning of such amounts as £3·41 and £1·03. In addition to the obvious use of coins, other apparatus such as number lines and structural blocks would be of help when introducing decimal fractions. It is suggested in the first instance that the decimal point used in expressing an amount of money is looked upon as a means of separating the pounds from the pence. A study of the work cards or manuals explaining the use of structural apparatus will indicate suitable methods to employ.

International system of units: S.I. units

Help children to be aware of the three units on which the system is based:

metre	m
kilogramme	kg
second	s

and other measures such as the litre for volume, ampere and volt for electricity, candela for light and Kelvin for absolute temperature. In the primary school we are concerned with temperatures in degrees centigrade (though for practical purposes the name Celsius has been adopted).

Decimal fractions

Use structural blocks and squared paper and give practical tasks to show counting in tens, i.e. ten units make a 'ten', ten 'tens' make a 'hundred', and so on. Tillach blocks, Dienes and Stern apparatus are useful for this.

Introduce a tenth part of a ten strip or rod as 0·1, two-tenths as 0·2, etc.

Then deal with hundredth parts of a hundred square expressed as 0·23, for example, not forgetting the importance of the nought, as in 0·04. Relate this to money, e.g. 23p as 0·23 of £1. Then deal with wholes and parts, e.g. 1·36, and £1·36 as one pound and thirty-six pence.

Length

Begin with centimetres marked on strips of paper, setting the children to measure different objects. Display metre strips horizontally and vertically with centimetres marked. Use as a number track and for children's heights.

Use strips of different lengths and fold for fractions, e.g. half a metre, quarter of a metre. When a length of less than a metre is measured, it is written using centimetres only, e.g. as 32cm. When the length is more than a metre, it is usually written in metres, e.g. 2·32m.

At first, consider the decimal point as separating metres and centimetres; later, relate it to decimal fractions. When more accurate measurements are asked for, introduce the millimetre as a tenth of a centimetre and later as a thousandth of a metre. Older children will need to know 3·265m as 3 metres and 265 millimetres, and a kilometre as 1,000 metres.

Weight

After the usual comparison of objects of varying weights, introduce the kilogramme as a standard weight. The gramme, too small for use in the primary school, should be considered in larger multiples, such as in half kilo, quarter kilo, 100g and 50g weights. Give plenty of experience in using balance scales, spring scales and levers, and in combining different units of weight to make up a given weight. The accent should be on the practical everyday use of weighing and the associated calculations necessary.

Capacity and volume

Give the children experience in filling litre measures with sand and liquids. Introduce half litres (500ml) and quarter litres (250ml). Let them graduate their own containers, using different shapes having the same volume. Lead them to discover that 1 litre is 1,000ml, which is almost exactly equal to 1,000 cubic centimetres.

Children may find difficulty in differentiating between capacity and volume. Point out that capacity, measured in litres and millilitres, could be considered as indicating 'space available', and is usually employed in the measurement of liquids; while volume, measured in cubic metres and cubic centimetres, could be thought of as 'space occupied', and is the measure used mainly for solids, although small quantities of liquids are sometimes measured in cubic centimetres. Help children to see the relationship between the millilitre and the cubic centimetre, the litre and the cubic decimetre. Give them practical experience so that they gain confidence in estimating and in using practical units.

Area

First use crude measures such as palms of hands, feet and tins. When a definite unit is required, centimetre squared paper is helpful. Introduce regular and irregular shapes. Use the centimetre squared paper in conjunction with cubic centimetre blocks. (A million cubic centimetres in a cubic metre will help children to see what a million is like!)

Time

Children first learn to tell the time by the hour, then the half hour, later the quarter hour, then by five-minute intervals, and lastly by the minute and half minute. Show them the twenty-four-hour clock, the times of which can be superimposed on a twelve-hour clock face, and explain that the twenty-four-hour day begins at midnight. All calculations of time are then so many hours and minutes past midnight.

The date, days and months as shown on the calendar should be taught. Include experiences which help in the appreciation of the passage of time. Very few written calculations in connection with time are needed in the primary school.

There is an increasing number of books on the market from which suitable examples for teaching the above measures can be chosen. Try to procure a few samples; then adapt the ideas and arrange the progression to the age and abilities of those you teach.

E RECORDING CHILDREN'S WORK

It is important that adequate records are kept of the work accomplished by each child and the progress made. The simplest but least meaningful way would be to indicate the subjects actually attempted, whether they involve different text books, work cards, structural apparatus, or projects. The items could be arranged in particular aspects of mathematics – number, money, length, etc. – and then each section further classified in order of difficulty. A record could then be kept of each area of work successfully completed. A record card or page in a record book might look like this:

	Work card						*Child's name*	*Age*
	1	2	3	4	5	6		
Number	√	√	√	√				
Money	√	√	√	√				
Length	√	√	√					
Weight	√	√	√					
etc.								

Where it is desired to include all the class on one sheet, the following layout could be used:

	Number	*Money*	*Length etc.*
	1 2 3 4 5 6	1 2 3 4 5	1 2 3 4 5
Irene E.	√ √ √	√ √	√ √ √
Mary P.	√ √	√ √	√ √
James F.	√	√	√ √
Timothy J.	√ √ √ √	√ √ √	√ √ √
etc.			

A far more meaningful and comprehensive record is that of the development of methematical understanding. The schemes of work should help with this, but it is difficult to determine an adequate progression. Not all children necessarily travel along the same path towards a true understanding of mathematics, but there are certain stages that one can note, and the order can be modified in the light of experience. Probably the best method is to base your record on the development of the real number system: collecting, sorting and classifying, matching, comparing, cardinal and ordinal numbers, counting and measuring; leading to the four rules of addition, subtraction, multiplication and division, and thence to fractional parts, reciprocals and the powers and roots of numbers.

The samples of record cards given here are outlines only and are meant as a guide. Selected items are shown in tabulated form for ease of recording. A tick should be placed in the appropriate box when the child has completed the work.

Explanation of record cards

Practical:

Experience: has used apparatus and been actively engaged in the task.

Understands: appreciates the function of the apparatus in this problem.

Recording:

Illustration: draws or makes diagrams, 3-D material, etc. to illustrate the experience.

Symbolic: uses symbols (in the early stages this column may not always be applicable).

Computation: abstracts the concept to use in calculations (additional column for juniors).

Sample of an Infant Mathematics Record Card

Name................................. Date of Birth..............

Activity	Practical		Recording	
	Experience	Understands	Illustration	Symbolic
Sorting and classifying objects into sets 1. On basis of *one* property, e.g. colour 2. On basis of *two* properties, leading to intersection of sets 3. On basis of *more than two* properties				
↓				
Division 1. Given number of objects in a set – how many sets? 2. Given number of sets – how many objects in each set?				
↓				
Time 1. Telling time – hour ½ hour ¼ hour 2. Calendar date days months 3. Passage of time				

Sample of a Junior Mathematics Record Card

Name................................ Date of Birth...............

Activity	Practical-Experience with Understanding	Recording	
		Illustration and Symbolic	Computation
Arithmetical laws Commutative: 1. Addition $a+b = b+a$ 2. Multiplication $a\times b = b\times a$ Non-Commutative: 3. Subtraction $a-b \neq b-a$ 4. Division $a\div b\neq b\div a$ Associative: 5. Addition $a+(b+c) =$ $(a+b)+c$ 6. Subjects related to addition if $a+b = c$ then $c-a = b$ and $c-b = a$			
↓			
Linear measurement 1. Crude measures 2. Standard measures: centimetre metre two at a time millimetres 3. Estimation 4. Approximation			

Chapter 8

Outline of Approaches to Some Other Subjects

It seems useful to include brief suggestions on the ways in which some other subjects can be tackled, namely: science and nature study, physical education, art and craft, and music. Religious education has been omitted purposely because there are so many conflicting ideas as to content and method and, in fact, on whether it should be introduced in the primary school at all! Most Education Authorities have produced detailed 'Agreed Syllabuses' for teachers to follow.

It is suggested that none of these subjects be thought of in isolation; the good teacher will find many opportunities for developing different themes or topics using a combination of subjects, in order to express ideas and situations which link these subjects together.

A SCIENCE AND NATURE STUDY

We are surrounded by nature. Consequently, of all the possible avenues of study, that of a child's natural surroundings is most likely to create the strongest impact. He can readily observe it, handle it and watch its development. Although there is no fine line of division, nature study can be said to be concerned with animal and plant life, and science with inanimate things. Until recently the former has taken precedence in primary schools, but the rapid advance of scientific knowledge and achievement has caused us to be aware of the necessity to establish a foundation of scientific knowledge, together with a systematic approach to examining objects and phenomena.

Nature Study

A good deal of nature study can be taught using specimens and objects brought by the children to school. They like to collect things, so it is not difficult to begin a nature table containing plants, flowers, nuts, seeds, etc., appropriate to the particular season. First of all a teacher should help with the naming of the specimens brought, and the printing of this information neatly on pieces of card to be placed next to the objects. An enterprising teacher will then find opportunities to talk about some of the material displayed and perhaps to encourage the children to produce a nature-science folder containing information and drawings.

It is important that children should learn to group objects together, because classification is a necessary part of scientific training. A suggested arrangement of nature samples on a table is as follows:

Specimens Never Alive	Live Specimens	Dead Specimens
Liquids e.g. water	Plants e.g. leaves, flowers	Plant remains e.g. coal, wood
Solids e.g. rock, metals	Animals e.g. small creature	Animal remains e.g. bones, feathers

Here can be seen the extension of the former 'nature table' to include inanimate objects. These displays provide an introduction to sorting and classifying by noting that the items belong to certain families or classes. The integration with mathematics and the language of sets will be noted. In the early stages children will readily note the set of animals and the set of plants. In addition, the display will help children to become aware of the existence of once-growing things such as peat, coal, wood, cork, etc., and of dead animals or parts of them, many of which things are to be observed in the countryside.

There is a vast amount of material for study which will capture the children's interests if suitably guided. Further classification of animals and plants can be a fascinating occupation. So too can a study of the growth of animals and plants, and their requirements for life: food, water and oxygen.

Nature study provides an opportunity for the teacher to help children to appreciate the beauties of nature and to learn to respect and care for living things. Nature walks, properly organized, can help to convey these attributes; at the same time they can be a source of inspiration, a time when a collection of specimens can be made, and an opportunity for the teacher to encourage observation.

A part of the school garden, tended by the children, will help them understand some of the ways in which things grow, and give them an interest which may be continued at home. The local park also offers many opportunities (see page 61 for further information).

Pets, mentioned in Appendix II, can also form a useful basis for scientific experiment; in each case, questions like these can be asked: How much food does it consume? What is its increase in weight over a given period (graph of this)? How long is its tail, its body, etc.?

Science

The nature-science table will contain materials under the 'never alive' section; the presence of these could, under the guidance of the teacher, lead to further scientific investigations and experiments. Materials such as magnets, wires, bulbs, batteries, wheels, corks, metals, bottles, etc., will appear if children are suitably encouraged.

But if a foundation of scientific knowledge and understanding is to be taught in a reasonable order of progression, it will be necessary to organize a series of experiments and investigations, particularly when the children reach junior school age. A teacher attempting this for the first time might appreciate a few notes on the preparation of material for simple science work. Do not in the early stages give science material to groups of children and expect them to discover for themselves. The result will be chaos. Prepare cards with precise instructions, indicating the apparatus needed and what to do with it. Later, when the children have become more sophisticated experimenters and observers, less instruction will be needed, and, in fact, some children may require little help from the teacher at all. But they do initially.

Try dividing the class into groups of not more than four, but preferably into pairs. Have a stock of cards suggesting experiments, in excess of those immediately required. Different experiments are advised for the simple reason that there will be economy in the use of apparatus if all are not doing the same task at the same time. One should mention, however, that not all teachers advocate the use of work cards and that some much prefer to allow the children to follow their own particular interests in science. For those who feel hesitant about how to tackle the organization of experiments that the children can do, here are some examples of work cards for various age groups:

Work cards for first year juniors

Batteries and Bulbs

You need: a bulb, a battery, pieces of wire.

1. Join the bulb to the battery using the wires so that the bulb lights up.
2. Draw what you have done.
3. Now remove the wires from the battery, turn the battery round and connect the wires in the opposite way.
4. Is there any difference?
5. Do the same with the wires connected to the bulb.
6. What do you notice?
7. Underneath your picture, write about what you did and what you found.

For older junior children a suitable experiment showing progression would be:

Science Experiment using Batteries, Wire, and Bulbs

What happens if you cut the wire?
Can you make a switch to make the light go on and off?
Connect two bulbs to the battery.
Using two batteries – does it make any difference how you connect them?
Make two bulbs light by connecting them in a different way (leading to series and parallel connections).

Air

Is there air in soil?

Things you need: a jar of water
a jar of soil.

What you have to do:

Slowly pour the water on to the jar of soil.
What happens? (Watch the top of the water.)
Say why you think this happens.
Write down the names of three animals which make passages in the soil, and therefore help the air to pass through it.

Work cards for second and third year juniors
(Note how the teacher makes use of the information in books)

Using a Magnet

You will need a magnet and the box of different things. (Objects, each of which is clearly marked, are wood, iron nail, cork, steel knitting needle, pen nib, comb, pencil, rubber, iron rod, etc.)

1. See how many of the objects in the box you can pick up using the magnet.
2. Try using each end of the magnet. Is there any difference?
3. Make two lists, one of things attracted and the other of things not attracted.
4. Write about what you did and say why you think some things are attracted to a magnet while others are not.
5. Try other objects in the room yourself, then find a book on the science table and read about other experiments you can do with magnets.

An Experiment About Moving Things

1. Read pages 6 and 7 in the book about Pulling.
2. Place the block of wood on the floor and try to pull it along with the string. Is it difficult?
3. Now try on other surfaces such as the playground, the corridor, the large piece of sand paper.
4. See whether the block is easier to pull if you put the marbles or round pieces of wood underneath.
5. Write about what you did and say what happened.

Work card for fourth year juniors

Clocks

(Use book *Primary Science Series*)
Work through the following experiments in your book:

1. Egyptian Water Clock.
2. Saxon Sinking Clock.

Write down the Roman numbers from 1 to 12
Read carefully pages 5 to 14.
Write about three different kinds of clock, name them.
How do they work?
Read page 15.
Answer questions 1, 2, 3, 4, 5 on page 16.
Write about your experiment using the following as a guide:

Title.
Things we needed.
What we did.
What happened and why.

Other ideas can be obtained from science books written specifically to help the young experimenter. It is possible for these books to be used instead of work cards by the teacher either suggesting certain sections to be read or allowing the children freedom of choice. Several books to help teachers are available. Mention must be made here of the valuable contribution to science teaching made by the Nuffield Foundation. A teacher would be well advised to study the Nuffield Science Books mentioned in Appendix V, and to use the many practical ideas and suggestions for experiments that are given.

Children's work should be recorded in some way, sometimes by diagrams only, usually by drawing and descriptive writing; or children could describe their experiment to others and explain what they discovered. A folder is useful for notes and is preferable to the conventional note book because it has a more flexible use. Sometimes it may be thought desirable to place together in one folder a series of notes about experiments done on a particular topic.

A useful pattern of recording is given here, but should not be strictly adhered to all the time. It is given as a guide:

Title.
Drawing or diagram of apparatus.
Description of what was done.
What happened or what was found.
What this shows or means.

As children become more proficient and confident in doing nature and science experiments, their interests will widen and the teacher will be challenged with such questions as these, which are selected from a list of those asked by some junior children:

Why does the liquid inside a thermometer rise up?
Why have clouds different shapes?
Why is iron colder than wood?
What causes a rainbow?
How does a fly walk on the ceiling?
How does fog come?
How does a fountain pen suck up ink?
Why do trees drop their leaves in winter?
If you swallowed a spider would you die?
Why does a spoon in a glass of water look as if it is bent?
What causes storms?

The questions are endless. We can only attempt to answer some, while leading the children to discover more for themselves.

Although in the early stages a separate science period may be necessary, science and nature study should not be considered in isolation from other subjects. Certainly, part of an English lesson could be spent writing science accounts, and pictorial representation is undoubtedly art.

We, as teachers, should aim at creating an interest in the environment and at helping the child to reconcile himself to it. We can do this, in part, by helping him to develop an enquiring mind and a purposeful scientific approach to the solution of his questions and problems.

B PHYSICAL EDUCATION

Planning a Lesson

The teacher of young infants, particularly of new entrants, needs to bear in mind that the introduction to P.E. must be done gradually and that not too much should be expected at first of the way in which apparatus is handled. She should be prepared to spend part of each lesson helping her class to become acquainted with simple commands and instructions. The vocabulary of movement is important; the children should be introduced to a variety of activities with corresponding verbal descriptions, for example: high and low, tall and small, to the left, to the right, above, below, light, heavy, strong, gentle, quick, slow, between, round.

Note also that children will not all have reached the same standard of physical development, nor will their rates of progress be the same. There will be the reluctant child who does not want to join in, and is content to sit and watch. It is advisable to allow this withdrawal at first, in the hope that after a while he will see how the others are enjoying themselves and gradually gain confidence to join them rather than be left out. A brief word of encouragement from the teacher or another child who has been enlisted to help should overcome shyness. This may continue for a lesson or two, so be prepared.

Some children like to be adventurous, so try to provide challenges for them. Balancing along a raised plank, swinging on fairly high apparatus, and climbing a rope ladder are suitable adventures which can be protected by the placing of soft mats to break a fall.

Rarely will a child slip or fall when allowed to accept the challenge of his choice. Gentle encouragement is preferable to pressure.

Much of what has been mentioned is applicable also to junior school children although, as their movements and body control become more sophisticated, the teacher will need to devise activities that cater for the skills and abilities beginning to develop.

The present-day approach to P.E. encourages more flexibility in the lesson, the incorporation of dance leading to drama, and an interrelation with other subjects such as art and music. However, there is still a need for lessons to be planned, but around a framework which can be flexible. A teacher should then draw upon his own ideas and those of the children, and attempt to interpret and develop the themes which arise according to the needs of the particular class. Guidance for a new teacher is therefore necessary; the following basic scheme is suggested:

First: General activity		
Then: Compensatory movements:		Leg and body
		Shoulder and arm
		Foot and leg
Thirdly: Agility movements		
	Part I:	Running
		Climbing
		Leaping
		Vaulting
	Part II:	Use of large apparatus

General activity

This is largely the children's own choice, but usually consists of running and walking at different speeds and in different directions, chasing games in small groups, and the use of small apparatus which the teacher should make easily accessible. Small apparatus is usually kept in baskets which will stack; it is advisable to have about half a dozen of them, each containing a selection of balls, skipping ropes, quoits, bean bags, bats, skittles, etc.

Compensatory movements

These are to compensate for parts of the body which may not often be exercised.

Leg and body. e.g. High kicking to touch outstretched hand; leg

movement while body is supported on shoulders and arms, hips in the air; leg swinging side to side and backwards.
Shoulder and Arm. e.g. Arm circling in different planes; crouch jumps; pulling body up a sloping bench.
Foot and leg. e.g. Throwing a ball or bag from between the feet; cat crawling; bouncing on feet with knees bent.

Agility movements
The items in the list speak for themselves. However, the list is by no means exhaustive and, as with the compensatory movements, items can be added or omitted according to the varying needs of the class.

Preparing Groups for Large Apparatus
Arrange the children in, say, eight groups, either with friends or as a random sample; e.g. all in one line, number 1 to 8, 1 to 8 and so on, then all the 'ones' in one group, all the 'twos' in another, etc. Each group is then allocated a corner or other space and is responsible for erecting a particular piece of apparatus.

However, it is suggested that the best way of introducing apparatus for the first time would be for the teacher to take a few children during lunch or break and to erect all the apparatus in certain prearranged places so that it is ready for the whole class. The children could then use it for a little while, and the rest of the lesson could be spent dismantling and erecting the various sections so that each group is reasonably proficient. This would minimize disciplinary troubles owing to delays when a full P.E. lesson is attempted.

The arrangement of course will depend upon the apparatus you have at your disposal. Use as much as possible of the space available and allow for a run-up to certain apparatus, such as the box and mats for agility. Where the arrangement for the activity is elongated, for example, in balancing on an upturned bench, attempt to have some other activity on the return journey, say a forward-roll on a mat, or passing through a hoop. (See diagram 10.)

The teacher should move from one group to another, encouraging and pointing out any outstanding feature of movement or initiative shown. Keep a watchful eye on the group attempting the most venturesome exercises, e.g. jumping over the agility box, and watch that children are aware of one another so they avoid crowding together.

When the teacher is satisfied with the first activity the groups can

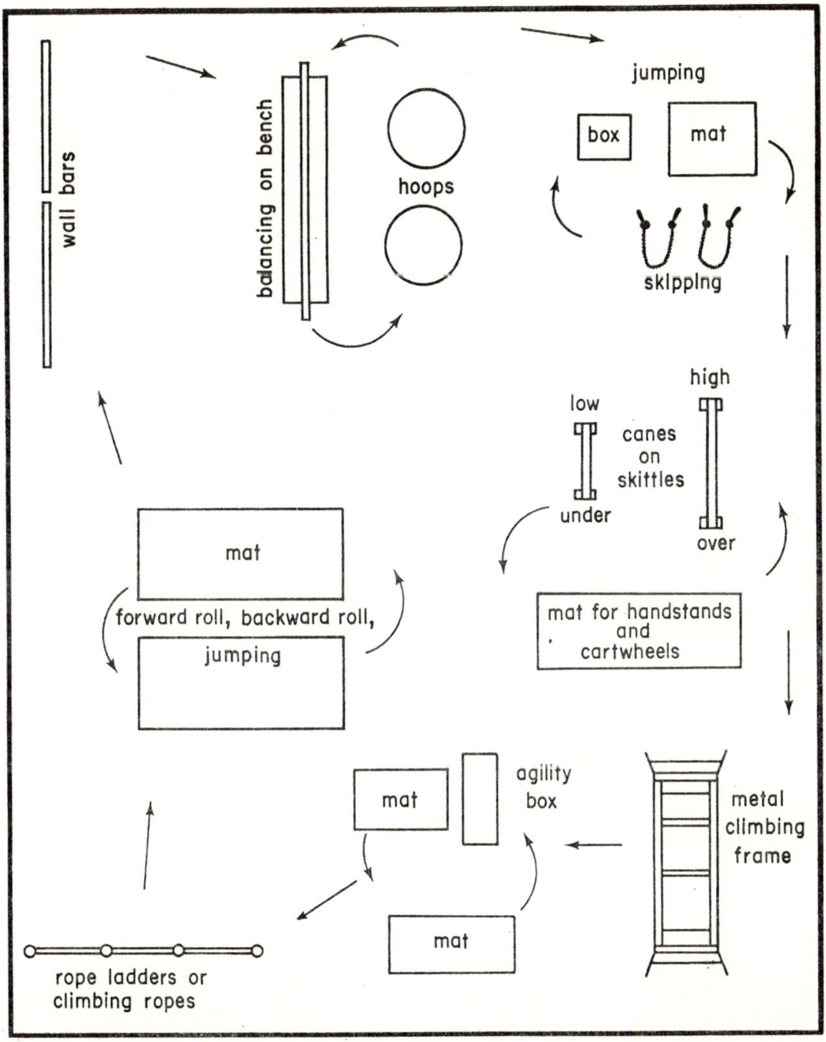

10. Plan of Hall showing Arrangement of Apparatus for P.E.
(Straight arrows indicate movement from one group to another.
Curved arrows indicate movement within a group.)

be allowed to move round the room to the next apparatus, thus enabling each child to sample all that is available. A point to watch in the arrangement of the apparatus is that there should not be two pieces of apparatus requiring similar abilities, e.g. strength of arms, next to each other. The child should encounter a variety of challenges as he passes from one section to another. Lastly, place mats in strategic positions in order to break falls or lessen the impact of landing.

Games

Games are very popular as a physical activity in the primary school. Younger children prefer to play with apparatus such as balls, bean bags, hoops, skipping ropes, by themselves or in twos or threes. Older infants and junior school children like to play games with others, but most of them are not ready for large team games such as football, cricket, netball or rounders until the last two years in junior school. Children need to become personally involved in the games they play and should be so guided that there is a progression in the development of such skills as throwing, catching, jumping, running, bowling, batting, fielding and kicking.

The small apparatus suitable for most of these activities can be stored in wire baskets which are then carried outside either by pairs of children or on a trolley. A selection of apparatus arranged in about six baskets will be found the most convenient, enabling all the class to move freely when collecting and replacing apparatus instead of converging on one point. It may be found convenient, however, to keep the medium-sized balls in one large basket. The same also applies to shinty sticks and long canes.

Begin a lesson with infants by allowing a free choice of apparatus but suggest certain activities to individual children. The next stage could be the practice of skills such as throwing and catching in pairs, followed by a game, say, team tag. There could be further use of apparatus, working in groups for such activities as balancing, skipping, jumping, landing and climbing.

With junior children there could also initially be the free choice of small apparatus, together with suggestions of activities at their level. Skills still need to be practised, so opportunities for batting, fielding, bowling and catching mentioned previously, should be given. Games such as the following could be arranged for children in groups of two, three, four or six: hitting a shuttle or a ball over a rope stretched between stands or two chairs; a game of shinty; heading a ball; bowling; batting and stumping (cricket or rounders style); dribbling a ball round several posts; throwing a ball into a bucket or netball net. A suitable conclusion would be a game of skittle-ball for some, six-a-side shinty for another group and volley-ball or stool-ball for the rest.

These notes about possible lessons have purposely been kept very brief because of the availability of other books dealing with this topic. Those indicated in Appendix V will show the wide variety of activities possible and will provide ideas for both the new and the experienced teacher.

Movement

Movement has already been mentioned in connection with drama. For the teacher unsure of this activity, the radio broadcasts of 'Movement and Mime' could be very helpful. Listen and Move records are also available, and a list of some suitable records is given in Appendix VI.

Initially, children should be helped to realize the space around them and to be conscious of one another and of the parts of their bodies which can move independently or together. Allow them to move to different rhythms produced by hitting a drum or tambourine. Introduce music that recalls or excites different feelings and allow the children to express what they feel. Mimes with or without music could develop and stories or happenings could be re-enacted. People and animals can be imitated, as can robots or machines; feelings can be expressed and sensitivity encouraged.

Here again, books dealing in detail with this particular topic are available. Please see Appendix V.

C ART AND CRAFT

The organization of art and craft should be such that it enables a child to express himself in the use of various materials, helping him to develop his senses of design, construction and decoration. The child should also find opportunities to develop his taste and judgement in appraising the artistic qualities of articles he sees every day. Therefore we need to provide a progressive development of skills which lead to independence in attempting individual work.

In the Infant School

Art and craft for infant children is really part of a wide variety of creative activities from which learning situations will develop. The young child begins to build and make models with wooden blocks and learns how to use constructional toys such as: Makimor, Leggo, Playstiks, screwing and fitting toys, jigsaw puzzles and, later, Meccano.

When painting and drawing, arrange for the children to wear old large shirts or provide them with plastic or rubber aprons, preferably with long sleeves and fastening at the front.

Give the children large sheets of paper; otherwise miniature paintings will result. Try various kinds, such as kitchen paper, cartridge paper, newspaper, wallpaper and sugar paper in a variety of shapes and colours. Younger children require powder paints of several different colours, ready-mixed to a fairly thick consistency with a separate brush in each colour. A liquid detergent plastic container is useful for such paint when the top has been cut off and inverted into the lower half. These paint holders can be secured in a wooden stand having holes the same diameter as a jam jar.

It is good for older infants to mix their own paints. Thick brushes size 10–12, are best but the more dexterous can use thinner ones occasionally to give extra detail.

Try finger painting, using powder paint and cold water paste on a non-absorbent paper. (Mix the paste first, then add powder to the required depth of colour.) Some children will also enjoy colouring with chalks on a large blackboard or sheet of dark paper. For drawing, supply thick soft pencils, wax crayons or charcoal.

When modelling, protective clothing is necessary if you wish to avoid visits from irate mothers complaining that a new blouse or shirt has been ruined. Plasticine has been mentioned elsewhere for modelling but other media are also worth trying. Dough, made by mixing two parts flour and one part salt (by weight) with water, can be modelled into various shapes and looks quite attractive when coloured with a vegetable dye. The salt of course preserves the dough. Clay is an excellent modelling medium but requires careful preparation and organization. To keep it at the right consistency, place it in a bin with a lid. If possible, have a small amount of water in the bottom of the bin and place the clay on a tray or piece of wood raised by bricks or blocks, so that the clay does not touch the water. This will keep the clay moist for several weeks provided it is covered with a damp cloth or plastic sheet. Roll the clay into small balls for storage. Be sure to cover the desks with a pastic sheet before use. Modelling tools can be purchased, but make use also of rolling pins, pastry cutters, etc.

Some children, particularly the boys, delight in using tools such as hammers, nails, saws and pinchers. If you are fortunate in having a woodwork bench, make good use of it by providing short lengths of soft wood and the necessary tools. If there is no bench, children could work on a large thick sheet of wood on the floor. It is important to make sure that tools are kept in good condition and stored in a definite place where they can be found.

Use can be made of various waste materials such as cotton reels, cardboard cylinders, wire, string, plastic containers, tins, lids, cheese boxes, corrugated paper, etc. From these, children can model railway engines, houses, furniture, motor cars, ships, puppets, rockets and animals.

Children enjoy cutting or tearing up coloured paper to make pictures. Old magazines make a useful source for this although very attractive coloured paper is also produced commercially. Good sharp scissors with rounded ends are the most suitable to use. Collages can be made by using a variety of materials having different textures. Scrap materials such as raffia, wool, feathers, leaves and buttons can be used, together with pieces of fabrics such as fur, cotton, ribbon, velvet and lace.

Older infants can sew, using simple patterns to make doll's dresses, covers for a doll's bed and small mats. Some could be taught to knit, using thick needles and wool with bright colours.

Cooking is a pleasurable and profitable occupation, particularly if a small cooker is available. Ingredients can be talked about, then bought from the local shops and costs calculated. They are then weighed and mixed together – this is always enjoyed. Oven temperatures can be mentioned (the teacher handling hot trays and shelves) and the required length of time for cooking measured. Buns for a party can be counted and allocated to several people. The learning situations produced will be obvious.

Children delight in taking home the things they have made, thus creating a link between home and school. This is particularly so at Christmas and Easter when small presents for parents can be made.

Junior Children

Much of what has been said already is equally applicable to art and craft in the junior school, particularly the remarks about protective clothing and the care and preparation of materials. Other suggestions concerning activities can readily be adapted and presented at a more advanced level so that progression is ensured.

The work requires careful planning and organization, but it is not necessary to be too rigid. Ideas should be flexible and children should be encouraged to develop their own creative instincts, rather than copy a particular exercise prepared by the teacher.

The ideal arrangement for art and craft work would be to have a section of a particular room, or a work bay as a working area. Part of a classroom could therefore be allocated to art and craft, and materials and tools placed in that area. Some teachers occasionally prefer all the class to be engaged in some form of art and craft at the same time; often there is a need for just a few children to be thus engaged, maybe as their contribution to a project, while others are writing or reading. Whichever idea is adopted, the arrangement of desks or tables in groups, to allow a large surface for the work, is desirable. This grouping also has the other advantage of enabling materials and paints to be shared. The entire surface should then be covered with newspaper or thin plastic sheeting to protect the wooden desks and tables. Some children could be responsible for giving out materials, which would ensure a prompt start, but all should be trained to clean and return the things they have used, leaving them tidy. It is better not to distribute water pots (jam jars usually) until actually required, because they are easily spilled; and they are always safer fixed in a block of wood or appropriate box. Junior children also require large sheets of paper of different colours and different media such as pastels, chalk, charcoal, etc. Collages can be made by having cloth materials for sticking on to pictures to give depth and texture.

Art and craft can and should be integrated with other aspects of the curriculum. Much valuable illustration and follow-up work can be achieved through pictures, diagrams and models. However, a good teacher will never lose sight of the fact that definite skills such as colour mixing, holding a brush, cutting, folding, designing, etc., need to be taught. Most of this teaching will be done incidentally, as and when a child requires that skill in order to accomplish a task satisfactorily.

Here are a few suggestions for those who have difficulty in deciding what to do:

Shapes and models using various media.
Composite models, e.g. farm, village, port, zoo, seaside.
Collection of leaves, shells, flowers, shapes, for arrangement and decoration of interest book.
Sketching objects of interest – part of local studies.
Character faces, e.g. clowns, witches, masks.
Use of two or more media at same time, e.g. wax and paint.
Lettering, handwriting patterns.
Imaginary birds, animals, fish.
Designing patterns from leaves, rubbings, odds and ends.
Printing – using sticks, fingers, potatoes, string, foam rubber.
Simple books – stitching, folding, decorating.
Book marks, Christmas cards, calendars.
Covers for exercise books, different sizes and shapes of books.
Concertina books, wallets, jotters.
Raffia work for table mats, slippers, coat hangers.
Weaving, using home-made cards; possibly a simple loom.
Clay modelling – copying shapes, animals, pots, faces.
Making puppets from rolled paper, or papier mâche.
Paper sculpture, e.g. flowers, leaves, masks, models, boxes, lanterns, buildings.
Woodwork – balsa wood models, use of other soft wood.
Cane work, e.g. simple trays, pot holders and baskets.

D MUSIC

Children should be helped to enjoy and appreciate music through listening, singing and playing, so encourage these activities in the hope that youngsters will become discriminating listeners and possibly interested performers. Ensure that the music you choose for your children is always of good quality.

To teach music really well is a job for the specialist, but the least musically inclined teacher can do quite a lot with a few aids and initiative. Try to be systematic, keep the children active and give variety, including singing, recorders, and percussion instruments. Recorder, pitched percussion and other instruments are usually available, so make good use of them.

All schools nowadays have a radio, so why not enlist this valuable aid which produces programmes made by experts? However, it is 'secondhand'; therefore it is necessary for a teacher to recapitulate some of the songs and to follow some of the suggestions so that children make their own music. Another very useful aid, which can be used in conjunction with the radio, is the tape recorder. Songs and music can be recorded and selections made for playing back as often as desired.

Singing

An enterprising teacher will attempt to learn at least the melody of certain tunes on the piano, recorder, guitar, xylophone or glockenspiel. The chromatic glockenspiel is easy to learn and gives quite good support to children's singing. Many teachers are quite proficient at using their own voices also.

Children enjoy singing, and enjoyment followed by interpretation should be the main aim. Younger infants like to sing nursery rhymes and other tunes having plenty of repetition which are within their vocal range. Older children should be introduced to traditional songs as well as to those of modern composers.

It is a good idea to begin a session of singing with a song the children know and like and to end in the same way. The songs you choose should have an appeal and be immediately attractive to the children. For those who have little idea of how to introduce a new song, a simple method is given below but there are other schemes which could be just as effective:

(a) Sing two or three verses to the children unaccompanied.
(b) Sing the first two lines unaccompanied. (Teachers with a limited singing voice will have to be content with playing the tune on an instrument or using a tape recorder.)
(c) Children sing first two lines to accompanying instrument.
(d) Repeat for the third and fourth lines.
(e) Sing and play the instrument with children for the whole verse.

Some people prefer to teach the verse as a whole. Experiment with both ways. If the song causes little difficulty, repeat the above with the second verse, but one or two verses would be enough at any one time. Add further verses in subsequent lessons.

Occasionally include instruments by asking the children which instruments would provide a suitable accompaniment. They might suggest, or be guided to suggest, triangles, say, for the first musical phrase, tambourines for the second, etc.; clapping and tapping could also be included. If possible, every child should have an instrument and be allowed to play in time with the rhythm of the song.

Playing Music

Children should also create their own music and explore the sounds that instruments make – and perhaps even make their own instruments, such as pipes.

A word ought to be said about pitched percussion instruments and their possibilities. A *xylophone* is made of wooden blocks, and gives a mellow tone with a rather short note. A *glockenspiel* is made of thin metal plates, the small type giving a high-pitched short note, the larger type, which has a resonator, giving a note which rings rather like a bell. *Chime bars* are also made of metal bars but usually each one has its own resonator consisting of a cylinder with a hole in it.

Each of the above can be played using two beaters, one in each hand. The beater is held lightly like a hammer and the notes are tapped using wrist movements.

It is often profitable to put out a few instruments in a corner of the classroom and to allow the children to improvise on them. Later choose simple repetitive music so that much of it can be learned by heart, thus enabling the child to keep his eye on the instrument – very necessary if the correct note is to be struck!

Allow children to experiment and to find certain sequences of notes with which they are familiar, e.g. parts of popular or traditional songs. Encourage them to listen carefully to the notes they play and to notice the different lengths of note, pitch and quality that are possible.

Then help them to discover notes that harmonize. Let the children make their own simple tunes of four or five notes in sequence at first, then write down the letters of the notes played. Words could be put to the tune, written underneath the notes and then sung while the instruments are played.

Children should soon be introduced to written music and shown how the notes 'climb' up and 'step' down the scale. Possible stages of progress when helping children to write down their own tunes could be:

1. Write down short phrases or sentences and put the note names underneath, e.g.

Run and jump with John and me.
C D E G D E C

2. Play and sing this, following the note names and words.
3. Add notes showing beat and values of notes.

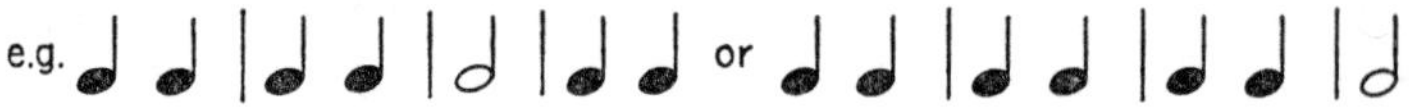

4. Transfer to the staff and play this music while watching notes and instruments. This is a big step and is often better done for the child, so that his enjoyment of the tune is not impaired.

Encourage the children to use pitched percussion instruments to accompany the songs they sing. Put two or three notes in the given key (as below) and ask the children to strike them in time with the song, or possibly in a slightly different rhythm. Then let them tap or clap the rhythm of words such as al-pha-bet, per-pen-dic-u-lar, or the rhythm of nursery rhymes and poems. When familiar with the pattern, they can tap or clap the rhythm, then beat it on the chime bars. In this way they can compose quite attractive tunes. If certain notes only are made available it will be impossible to play disharmonies.

Some correct combinations to avoid discordant notes are as follows:

C	D	E	G	A	(Pentatonic scale of C)
D	E	F♯	A	B	(Pentatonic scale of D)
F	G	A	C′	D′*	(Pentatonic scale of F)
G	A	B	D′	E′*	(Pentatonic scale of G)

Similar arrangements can be made using xylophones and glockenspiels. The children find it easier if the notes are clearly marked and if all notes not needed are removed.

The *descant recorder* has a very mellow note when played well.

* C′, D′, E′ are played in the octave above the middle-C octave.

The Schott wooden descant and the Dolmetsch plastic descant recorders will be found quite satisfactory for primary children. Wooden ones can split and plastic ones crack easily if dropped, so the choice is yours. Wooden recorders should not be allowed to become moist – shake gently while keeping a firm grip. Some suitable books are indicated in Appendix IV.

Listening to Music

Listening to music needs to be for short periods only, the length depending on the age of the children. Two or three minutes are quite long enough for infant children with frequent repetition and participation in the form of body movements. The length of time for older children can be increased gradually. There will, of course, be quiet periods encouraged by appropriate music.

The record player, available in all schools, can be put to good use as there is a wide choice of suitable recorded music. A small sample is listed in Appendix VI.

Instruments of the orchestra can be discussed, pictures shown if actual instruments are not available, and their sounds picked out while listening to various musical compositions. Do not attempt to run through all the instruments of one group, e.g. strings, woodwind, percussion, but pass from one group to another, e.g. the violin the first time, the violin again the second time, followed by, say, the trumpet. Suitable instruments might be: violin, cello (strings); flute, clarinet, bassoon (woodwind); horn, trumpet, trombone, tuba (brass); timpani, side drum (percussion). Taped music is best for this kind of lesson because one can readily choose a particular part to play.

Some BBC programmes found suitable are:

'Music Corner'	Infants
'Music and Movement'	Infants
'Time and Tune'	Top infants, first year juniors
'Music, Movement and Mime'	Juniors
'Music Workshop'	Juniors
'Singing Together'	Juniors

Chapter 9

Some Additional Responsibilities

A ASSESSMENT OF CHILDREN

Examinations and Record Cards

It is important that we observe and record the interests, abilities, attainments and progress of the children in our schools.

Examinations and tests are very limited in their effectiveness, mainly because their validity is often impaired by the inadequacy of the test itself and by emotional factors affecting those being tested. Educators are becoming increasingly aware of the value of teacher assessment which, when done with insight and understanding, can produce a truer picture of a child's abilities and attainments, because the teacher can observe him over a long period. Nevertheless, personal judgement is not infallible so a combination of test results and personal assessment would appear to be the answer.

Education Authorities usually require a record card to be kept for each child and many schools have devised cards or booklets themselves. There are usually spaces for internal and external test results, personality assessments, home background and family history, and health.

In order to be in a position to help a child who is new to school we need to know something of his home background, previous illnesses which may have affected him physically, e.g. in sight and hearing, and experiences he has had which may affect his reading and other school work. As he progresses through the school it will be necessary to note the standards reached in reading, writing and mathematics, and characteristics such as sociability, self-confidence, application and temperament.

A junior record card will also indicate internal and external tests. The latter will consist mainly of intelligence test results. Teachers' assessments of both attainment and personal qualities such as perseverance, artistic ability, practical ability, reasoning, speed of work, etc., will also be shown. There will be space for comments on family background, illnesses, and any physical defects.

Sample of an Infant Record Card

Name: *Address:* *Date of Birth:*

Progress in Mathematics:

Reading:
Age (when chron. age is 6+)
Progress

Written Expression:

General:
Sociability
Self-confidence, application to work, etc.

Health:

Home:

Sample of a Junior Record Card

Name:	*Address:*	*Date of Birth:*
Position in Family:	*Previous school:*	
Attendance:		
Qualities and Aptitudes: e.g. Perseverance Sociability Pace of work Self-confidence	 Oral expression Verbal ability Practical ability Artistic ability	
Disabilities: e.g. Eyesight Hearing	 Instability Nervous disorders, etc.	
Intelligence Test Scores:		
Record of School Work: (for each year of half year, usually position in age group, with comments). Mathematics English Other subjects		

The qualities and aptitudes are usually assessed on a three- or five-point scale, that is, A represents excellent, B good, C average, D poor and E very poor, comparing within the same age group. Where a record of school work is indicated there is little point in showing scores or percentages as these can be very misleading. For instance, if an easy test is given most children will have very high scores; the converse is true also. A much truer representation is to indicate a child's position in relation to others or, perhaps better still, his percentile score.

It is a good plan to keep your own assessment book with a page for each child. There will not be any reason to add to it each day but it is useful to note certain stages or achievements of children as they are observed.

B MEETING PARENTS

Parents are welcomed in most schools providing lessons are not interrupted. The amount of contact the school has with parents will be determined by the head teacher, so general comments only can be made here.

If there is a Parent–Teacher Association at the school opportunities to meet parents may occur frequently. Unfortunately the parents who do not attend the meetings are those you most need to see because, on the whole, their children are less keen and make less progress than the children of parents who take a genuine interest in the school. On the other hand, parents will be very anxious to attend functions where their offspring are taking an active part. Concerts and carol services with nativity plays are very popular. So too are evenings when children's work is displayed and they can bring their mothers and fathers to look around. You may find this is your only chance to speak to some parents.

Many schools organize Parents' Evenings when they can come to school to look at their children's work and discuss their progress privately with the teacher. If this happens in your school, arm yourself with brief notes about each child and underline a few points you may wish to make and questions you might wish to discuss with your head teacher with a view to mentioning to parents:

Does he/she read much at home? Mention school library, local library, borrowing books; recommend books.

Does he/she like school? Importance of good relationship between home and school, your readiness to co-operate.
What is he/she like at home? Interests, personality.
Any problems with health? Mention particular illnesses, eyes, hearing, where appropriate.
How parents can help: reading to the child
listening to his reading
helping him to choose good books
spending plenty of time with him, talking and explaining things
encouraging interests
encouraging school work, follow-up
times of going to bed, T.V. times
Homework (if any given) value, how much parent should help.
Encouragement to contact school again if any problems, or perhaps just for interest.
Explain how to make appointments.

It is the writer's belief that we as teachers should always be honest with parents about the progress and behaviour of their children. Do not condemn, however, in front of the child. We should try to be objective in our assessment of standards, both achieved and expected.

C REPORTS TO PARENTS

It is likely that you will be required to make certain comments on children's work in a report prepared for parents. Here again be honest, but also careful, straightforward and clear. Far from clear are the remarks 'average', 'fair', 'only fair', 'very fair', 'needs to concentrate more'. An 'average' score is the sum of all the scores divided by the number of scores, so there can really only be one average score anyway; and is there ever an average ability that can be considered, and of what is it the average? 'Fair' is an even less meaningful remark and is probably used when the assessor cannot think of anything positive to say. A teacher might profitably avoid the 'lacks concentration' remark because this could easily be interpreted as self-condemnation of a teacher's ability to create suitable learning situations.

Much preferable to the above are more detailed and well considered remarks indicating the levels achieved and difficulties overcome.

Most parents want to know how their children are progressing in relation to others and how much they have improved on their previous performances. Comments on a report to parents of an infant might be:

> Bill's progress in mathematics is very encouraging.
> He readily sorts and classifies objects and has begun to record little sums about his activities. His progress in reading is slightly better than that of other children his age.

Or:

> His progress has been slower this term but he has managed to read his first small book, so we are hoping that with regular practice he will soon be able to build many words himself.

Part of a report to parents of a junior child might read:

> John has found difficulty in settling down since he started in the junior department but we are very pleased that he now joins in all activities including P.E. He has not progressed as well as we could expect in reading but his understanding of number is better than most others in the class.

Or:

> Simon has now mastered the mechanics of reading and should be encouraged to read widely by borrowing books from school and possibly becoming a member of the local library. He takes a great deal of interest in the geographical and historical facts of the area. This is helping his written expression which has improved greatly this year. Drama is one of his strong points and he has written a play that some of the class have performed.

When there is adequate contact between home and school, much information about a child can be conveyed verbally. Also, there is the advantage that, knowing the parents, the teacher can vary the information and wording on a report to suit particular needs.

Chapter 10

On Tape and Film

A USING A TAPE RECORDER

Most schools now have tape recorders, but unfortunately not all put them to good use. There are probably two reasons for this:

(a) many teachers are apprehensive about being able to master the mechanics of the tape recorder; and
(b) teachers are not always aware of the educational possibilities that a tape recorder presents.

It is possible for most teachers to become proficient in the manipulation of the controls; older children too are often capable of understanding how to stop and start the machine and even to record.

Tape recorders differ so much that it is impossible to give precise instructions that would suit every machine. However, there are certain basic rules to follow and, having noted these, a teacher would be well advised to read carefully the instruction booklet supplied with the tape recorder. Let us assume that you are given the machine and a spool bearing a tape on which a wireless broadcast has been recorded. First of all, place the spool of tape on the left hand spindle so that it rotates in an anti-clockwise direction as the tape is removed. Unwind a short length of tape, hold the end in your right hand and, at a place about 30 cm from the end, hold the tape with the left hand. Then, holding it taut, slot the tape into the sound channel. The shiny side should be towards you.

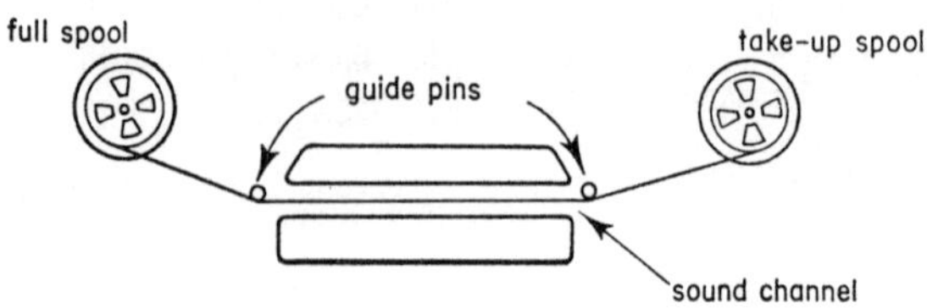

11. Tape Recorder Deck.

Wind the tape on to the take-up spool, on the right hand spindle, in an anti-clockwise direction until it overlaps, using the slot in the spool to help you. You should now be able to wind the tape on to the) take-up spool by hand, feeling a slight resistance. (See diagram 11.) The next task is to plug into the mains and switch on. There may be a volume control knob on the tape recorder which also switches on the mains supply. You are now ready to press the key or turn the knob marked *start*. Regulate the volume control to your liking. The operation of the stop key or knob should need no explanation. The tape may be rewound on to the original spool by operating the appropriate key or knob, usually clearly marked.

Before recording from the radio or a microphone turn down the output volume control, otherwise you will get a high-pitched note from the speaker, and plug the lead into either the radio or microphone socket on the tape recorder (these are sometimes at the back or side). In order to record, turn the knob to *record* or, as on most machines, press the knob marked *record* (usually red) and at the same time press the *start* key. If the machine has a record-level figure, the figure indicated (usually in the red section) must not be exceeded when the highest recorded volume is heard; and when the tape recorder has a valve with two lights to indicate the record level, these must not overlap. It is not always possible to arrange for the microphone to be close to the performer, but the best distance is about twenty-five to fifty centimetres away.

Some Practical Suggestions

The most common use to which the tape recorder is put is the recording and playing back of radio broadcasts. By so doing, suitable programmes can be stored to be played back at a time more convenient or appropriate. In addition to this there is a great advantage in being able to stop a programme at any part in order to discuss a point or to repeat a particular secton. It is possible for teachers, and even children to produce their own programmes of instruction, and perhaps to compile a recorded magazine for replay to the class or school.

The tape recorder encourages a child to listen critically to his classmates and to himself. It encourages correct oral expression and creative work in drama. The following are some suggestions for recording:

Recording aloud, playing back to oneself.

Describing objects in the room or while out walking, then replaying and perhaps writing about or painting.

Giving a running commentary on, for instance, a football match.

Interviews with visitors to the school, with people who have a particular job, e.g. policeman, postman, caretaker.

Imaginary interviews with imaginary people.

Children telling stories either remembered or composed by themselves.

Recording of visits and expeditions.

Recording of music made by children so that it can be appraised.

An introduction to part singing, or rounds.

You may find it worth-while to experiment later with the use of the tape recorder as an aid in programming a series of lessons for helping children to read, develop the understanding of number, etc. The use of earphones as extensions would allow children to work with the tape recorder in a classroom without disturbing others.

B USING A FILM-STRIP PROJECTOR

Film-strips consist of a series of pictures in sequence on a length of film. The film-strip can be used in its entirety at any one time or, more usually, only those sections of it which are particularly appropriate.

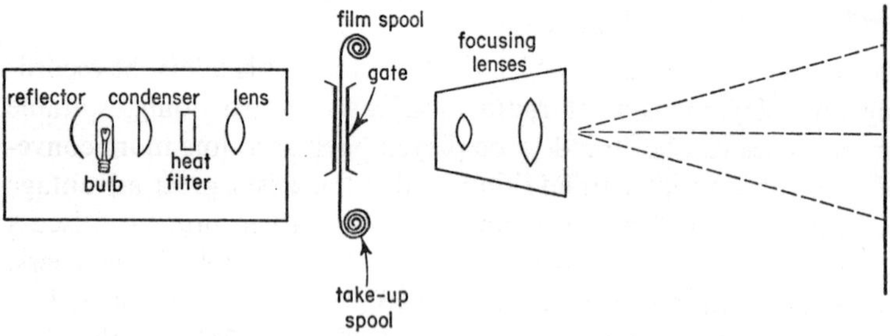

12. Film-strip Projector Parts.

The essential parts of the projector are shown in diagram 12.

The light from the bulb passes through the lens and gate holding the film. The front lenses focus the image on the screen.

Loading

Take the film-strip from its box and unwind it a little so that a few frames can be seen. While holding the strip up to the light, look for some writing. You must alter the position of the strip until the writing in the frame is the correct way up and can easily be read. Next, turn the strip until the writing is upside down, taking care not to reverse the film back and front (diagram 13). The arrow in the

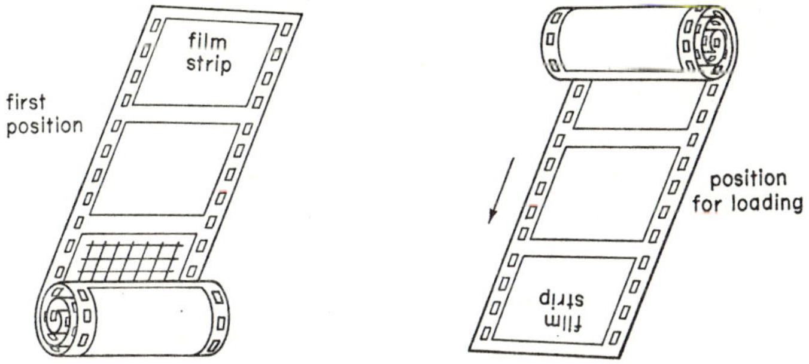

13. Loading a Film-Strip (1).

figure on the right of diagram 13 shows the direction in which the strip will pass through the gate of the projector.

You now need to unwind all the film until you come to the end, thread the *end first* on to the film-strip holder (diagram 14) which should first be unclipped from the projector. The holder usually just pulls off.

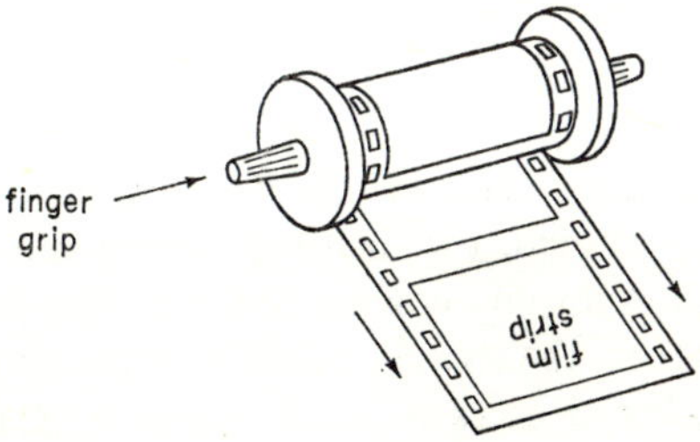

14. Loading a Film-strip (2).

Having wound the strip backwards on to the holder, clip the holder on to its spindle on the projector, ease the gate forwards by pushing forward the small finger grip of the film-strip holder, and pass the strip through the gate (diagram 15). Now, clip the film into the take-up spool and wind it on for a couple of revolutions. You are now ready to project.

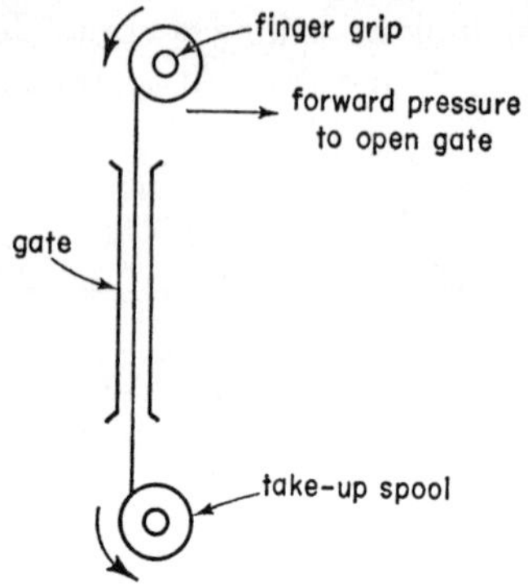

15. Loading a Film-strip (3).

Projecting

Plug into the mains and switch on the projector. Place the screen initially about five metres from the projector. You should now see a blurred image on the screen. If you cannot see anything, turn the second film-strip holder so that the film winds on a little. In order to focus the image on the screen, turn the front lens housing until the picture is clear and you have a crisp image. The best focusing is done using either printed words or the special focusing frame which contains lines running in various directions. This frame is found at the beginning of most film-strips. You may need to alter the distance between screen and projector so that the picture just fills the screen. If this distance is altered, the focusing will have to be re-set.

The best position for an audience to see a clear picture from is at least two metres from the screen and within an angle of sixty degrees, that is within thirty degrees on each side of a straight line drawn from the centre of the screen to the projector (diagram 16). This amount will vary slightly according to the screen used.

Avoid switching the bulb on and off while it is warm and never move the projector until the lamp has cooled. Careful attention to these two points will certainly lengthen the life of the bulb.

If you ease the gate forwards slightly when moving to the next frame, this will prevent possible scratching due to small particles of grit finding their way between the two pieces of glass in the gate of the projector.

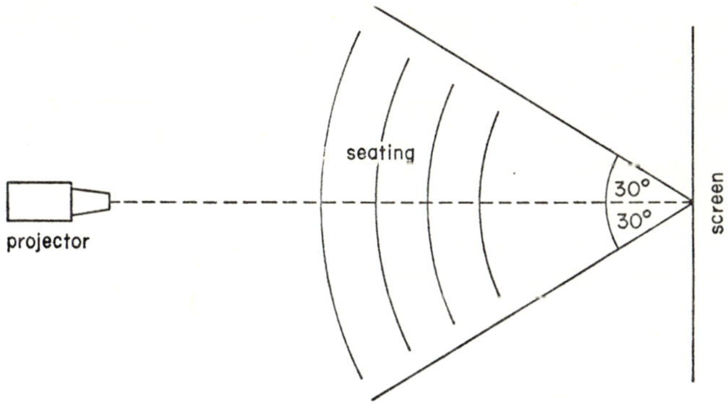

16. Seating Arrangements for Screening.

When you have finished, carefully wind the end of the film-strip on to the second holder, remove it from its spindle and unwind the strip, taking care not to touch the pictures with the fingers. The strip can then be rolled to an appropriate size for its box.

Film-strip projectors with automatic loading are also available; the modified loading technique should be described in the manual of instructions.

When a projector is used to show slides or transparencies, the film-strip gate has to be removed and replaced by a slide carrier. The other principles mentioned above still apply.

Appendix I

Examples of Children's Writing

PROSE

Inspiration: The moon landing.

We are Going to the Moon
We are going to the moon and capsules are on it too. and we are going to go on the moon and a rocket is on a launching pad. 87654321 ignition. The rocket went up and a man saw it and he was in the woods. A man jumped on it and he saw the earth the earth was blue and he saw a house and a boat and a tree and a car . . . when you go to the moon you can see the space station and you can see TV in the rocket and in the space station and a rocket has three parts the end.

Tyrone aged 6

Inspiration: Talks and displays about far northern countries.

Eskimos
It is just about dawn in Greenland and at 1 o'clock in the morning Sercok went to catch a big whale. It was so big that the Eskimos dive at it. They had part of it for breakfast it was delishas, then there was a smash crash rumble and roll and there was a thunder storm but they went in the igloo.

Nichola aged 6½

Inspiration: Dressing up, talks about people who help us.

When I Grow Up
When I grow up I want to be a nurse and Ill help sick people and look after them. Ill give them baths and at breakfast time Ill give them breakfast and at dinner time Ill give them their dinner. After I will give them their tea and tuck them into bed and draw the curtains then go round the ward to see if little girls and boys are

asleep. If a baby cries I will go and pick them up and feed them then put them back in their cots and in the morning I will give them their breakfast.

Jayne aged 7

Inspiration: Visit to a local farm.

We went to Mr. Morgan's farm yesterday afternoon. First of all we went to see where the cows were milked. Before you go into this place there is a place where all the names of the cows are. There are 140 cows, there are 30 Jersey and 110 friesien. the tops on the Jersey cows milk were gold and the tops of the friesien were silver. The Jersey cows milk was much creamier so it was dearer.

When we were in watching the cows being milked I saw that one cow had 40 pints of milk and another had 24 pints so the first had 16 pints of milk more. There was a big metal thing where the milk ran down and then went into some pipes and into a churn.

The cows ate a kind of cake and they liked it very much. They only eat the cake when they are milked so they like getting milked. I liked watching the cows getting milked best.

Shane aged 7½

Inspiration: Nature talks, radio broadcast, books.

How Tadpoles Grow
In a lonely part of the pond mother frog lays her eggs. The frogs eggs are called frog spawn. Mother frog leaves her eggs on their own. If you think the eggs have some protection you are right. Frog's eggs are smothered with jelly.

Soon a tail grows and it turns into a different shape. After about ten days it grows two legs. After a while it grows front legs and loses its tail. Then it grows into a frog. Then it hops out of the water and sits in the sun.

Caroline aged 8

The following is an example of an alternative to note copying or recall of information imparted. Here the child is more involved.
Inspiration: Holidays, sea shore collection, talks with teacher.

The Starfish

'Hello my name is Jack the Starfish. I have five arms with millions of sucker feet. I have red beads at the end of each arm which are my eyes. Some people call me Five-fingered Jack. Sometimes when an enemy bites an arm off, a new arm grows and if that bitten arm is left to float about the sea it grows four more arms. I like to eat mussels and limpets and if the limpet is stuck to the rock I pull and pull and pull until it comes off. Then I crack the shell open and squirt some poison in the shell so the limpet is forced to come out and be eaten. I live in a rock pool with a few other starfish who are in my family. One day a little girl saw me and took me home to show me to her uncle.'

David aged 8

Here again the child puts herself into the story, but this time there is no recall of facts learned.

Extract from *My Day Of Freedom*

My name is Prince. I am a guard dog at Maple Tree Farm. . . . I lay down again but did not sleep. It was dusk. I felt a ripple of uneasiness run down my spine. The village clock struck ten o'clock. I heard the crackle of twigs. I was on my guard immediately. If I heard anyone at the farm I had to listen intently and pounce if it was anyone strange. Now I was on my own in the dark wood without the comfort of thinking the farmer was in bed and all I had to do was to bark to bring him hurrying down the stairs.

The person came nearer and nearer. He, if it was a he, smelt strange in some way. I slunk away quietly so that I could pounce. An agonizing cry came from the man – I had bitten his leg. . . .

Judith aged 10½

Imaginative account after class discussion, reading of poetry and dramatization:

Fear

It is a wet gloomy dark night. My Mother and Father have gone out I feel very scared. When are Mother and Father coming home? What if they don't come back? A noise, what was it? I will look out of the window. A shadow, oh what was it? Oh my skin has gone tight. Oh a shiver down by back. A car. I sit. Mum and Dad? The stairs are creaking who is it? The door is opening who is it? Mum hasn't got a red dress like that. It might be a stranger, oh no. Oh it is only the wind I will shut it. it is very cold. It is very dark now, so I will get into bed. Oh what is that on my foot? Oh it is only my gown (ding dong) who is that? I will go downstairs and see. Oh Mum Dad if is you, I thought that some one was opening the door but it was your night dress hanging on the line in the hall, well come in.

Tracey aged 9½

A different slant on the writing of an historical account, where the child is asked to put himself in the place of an individual living in the past:

I Was There
It was the year 1066 and we were going to be invaded by the Normans. We had just fought one battle against the Danes. So we were very weary and now we had to go on a great long walk which would make us even more weary. But we started our long walk. We found a forest and sheltered in it, we were all very tired. While we were resting some of William's scouts were out and they saw us, so they went back and told William. So they were ready for us. When it was morning we went on. We saw the Normans, so we went up on to a hill. Then the Normans were ready. We had made a steel wall with our shields then battle began. They threw spears and the stones out of their slings. The archers fired their arrows that just hit against our wall or just sped over our heads. At last they charged but we beat them down again. Again and again they charged but every time we beat them down again. But the next time they charged some of us broke the wall so they got through. And we were soon being beaten. The noise was deafening. Suddenly King Harold was killed so now we knew that we had lost the battle.

Martyn aged 9½

Inspiration: Personal investigations, group and individual work.

Encounters
Here are some of the better encounters I have had. I was walking

one day in a marsh when I heard a thin reedy piping coming from a clump of rushes. I flushed the clump of rushes and to my surprise a common shrew came walking out of the rushes. It was very frightened, so after I had given it a thorough examination I replaced it on the ground.

The second encounter was not expected and I was not looking for what I found. I was walking along the cliff top at Goodrington when I saw something gleaming on the bank. When I got nearer I could hardly believe my eyes, for there, on the path was a young sloworm with its tail amputated. Every lizard can drop it's tail when it is alarmed, and as the sloworm is a legless lizard, with a notched not forked tongue, it was no exception. The third encounter was just as unexpected as the last one, and was on the same day, on the same beach. I had noticed some strange triangular holes in the sand, and just passed them by. But when we dug round one, everyone was surprised, for there, lying in the hole, was a sea urchin. These sea-urchins are quite common on Goodrington beach, and for the rest of the day we dug up twelve or more. I noticed that all these sea urchins had a strange habit of burrowing themselves into the sand. They do this by moving their spines and gradually scraping the sand away.

William aged 11

POETRY

An early attempt at poetry writing (lines arranged by teacher):

In the country the leaves dance all day.
The sun shines down upon the trees
which makes them grow to the bees
flying in the trees,
and the people love the shady trees
if it is a hot day.

Jonathan aged 6½

Inspiration: Season of autumn, collection of fruits and leaves, stories of creatures and what they do in autumn, poems, nature walk.

The Insects in Autumn

Good night said the spider climbing into bed,
Good-bye said the wasp flying away,
Oh dear said the bee I am a sleepy head,
Oh dear said the ant it's autumn today.

Animals in Autumn

The squirrels hop about looking for nuts,
The little brown beaver making little huts,
A little white rabbit is curling up to sleep
The hedgehog lies in a prickly heap,
The tortoise pops into his house,
Good night good night says the little mouse.

both by Sharon aged 8½

Autumn

What are the colours of Autumn?
Red, brown, yellow and gold.
Where are the birds all flying?
To warmer lands we are told.
Where are the squirrels hiding?
Cosy in their dreys,
And till the springtime comes again
Thats where the squirrel will stay.

Jane aged 9

Inspiration: Poems about small creatures, paintings, discussion, – religious education?

Tiny Things

The tiny fly
That seldom comes nigh,
The dandelion like a feather bed,
The sunflower tall
Climbing the garden wall,
The daisy shy
Watching the busy bee go by;
The buttercup like gold
Looking bold;
God made these things for us
Because we're the ones he loves.

Janet aged 10

Inspiration: Talk and film about an Australian sheep station.

The Shearing Barn
The sheep are struggling, bleating, weaving,
Outside the barn a boy is heaving
An old scraggy ewe into the shed,
Where the shearer is waiting, impatiently shouting.
The ringer last time by chance cut a sheep
But the tar boy was ready to put tar where it bled.
At last when the wool is packed up for market,
The shearer goes wearily back to his bed.

David aged 8½

Inspiration: Poems, talking about the wind.

House on the Hill
It was a lonely place
On top of that green hill,
It was all so quiet
And ever so still.
Then came the wind
And bellied out the clothes
And the shirt landed
On the little pig's nose.

Then they came back
And puffed out once more
With the wind in their limbs
They blew and they tore.

Claire aged 8½

Appendix II

Classroom Animals

MORE ABOUT CLASSROOM PETS

Apart from the delight and enjoyment which the study and care of animals can give to children, they help to create a sympathy towards smaller living creatures and can be the basis of simple lessons in biology.

Further, some pets can be weighed and measured and the increase noted and graphed; consumption of food and drink can be determined. Pets can also be a source of inspiration for art and descriptive English and, with young children new to a school, could be a means of reconciliation to the different surroundings.

GUINEA PIGS, HAMSTERS AND RABBITS

These are all pets to handle and stroke. Keep them in a wooden box with two compartments, one having wire-netting at the front. Put sawdust on the floor and make beds of straw. Clean out every two days.

Food consists mainly of oats and vegetables; rabbits also like pellets which can be bought from the pet shop. Other suggested foods are: clover, dandelion, beetroot, sprouts, carrots, cabbage, lettuce, swede, apples and most fruit. Avoid buttercups, bluebells, anemone, deadly nightshade, marigolds, potato tops, horse-chestnuts.

A healthy rabbit has a glossy coat and bright eyes. An unhealthy rabbit can have: too much fat on its backbone, canker in the ear, eczema sores, 'pot belly'.

A healthy hamster or guinea pig has bright eyes and perked ears, and is lively and plump. Buy one about eight weeks old if you can. An unhealthy hamster might have: bare patches in its fur, scars on its body, small spots near the ears or nose.

GERBILS

A pet to be handled, A gerbil is a small rodent with a long tail.

K

Some of the wilder ones will bite fingers. It needs a cage similar to a hamster, but might gnaw the side. These animals are odourless and clean. Attention and food required are similar to those for a hamster.

CANARIES AND BUDGERIGARS

Procure as large a cage as possible. Have a sandpaper tray on the floor of the cage and clean out twice a week. Feed on seeds and millet and give a little cuttle fish for sharpening beaks. Have a water trough for drinking and bathing.

GOLDFISH

These pets require very little care. Provide a large rectangular tank. If only a bowl is available, only half-fill it, to provide a larger area of water to absorb air. Give them only a pinch of food every two days. Avoid over-feeding. Algae may form when the bowl is in too much light; if this happens, place it in a position away from direct sunlight.

TROPICAL FISH

Fish of this kind are much more attractive, but require more attention; also, the provision of a tank and accessories could be expensive. It is necessary to keep the water in the tank around 24 degrees Centigrade and for this a heater and thermostat are required. It is advisable to read a book about tropical fish before embarking on this venture. The water must be aerated either by tropical plants or an aerator pump. Feed with a pinch of tropical fish food each day and with tiny worms or chopped meat occasionally.

Introduce new fish by floating the plastic carrier-bag provided in the tank for about ten minutes before releasing the fish; this balances the water temperature.

A WORMERY

If the recognized wormery, consisting of sheets of glass a few inches apart with strips of wood at the ends for support, is not available, a large jar or bowl will suffice.

Place a layer of sand at the bottom, then gravel, then soil, and top with a layer of leaves. Place black paper around and on top of the bowl to keep out the light. The worms will then come to the sides where their movements can be seen. It is necessary to dampen the soil occasionally with water.

Appendix III

A Few Poems Found Suitable for Various Age Groups

YOUNGER INFANTS

'My Donkey', transl. Fyleman R.,
'Jellical Cats', Eliot, T. S. etc.: *Book of Nursery Verse* (Faber).
Number rhymes: *Number Rhymes and Finger Plays*, Boyce, E. R. and Bartlett, K. (Pitman).
Traditional nursery rhymes: *Oxford Nursery Rhyme Book* (Oxford U.P.).
'The Scarecrow', Farjeon E.,
'Shadows', Farjeon, E., etc.: *Tom Tiddler's Ground.* Chosen by De la Mare, W. (Collins).
Traditional nursery rhymes: *The Land of Nursery Rhyme* (Dent).
Traditional nursery rhymes: *The Mother Goose Treasury* (Hamish Hamilton).
'The Three Foxes',
'Market Square',
'Missing',
'Rice Pudding', etc. *When We Were Very Young*, Milne, A. A. (Methuen).

OLDER INFANTS

'The Snowman', Adams, E. M.: *Come Follow Me* (Evans).
'Sneezles',
'Down by the Pond', etc.: *Now We Are Six*, Milne, A. A. (Methuen).
'The North Wind Doth Blow', Anon.: *Puffin Book of Verse.*
'Topsy Turvy',
'My Tom Cat',
'Mr All-Sorts',
'Nancy Nibs', etc.: *The Ladybird Book of Bedtime Rhymes* (Wills & Hepworth).
'Hailstones and Halibut Bones', O'Neill, M.: *The World's Work.*

'Sand Between the Toes',
'The King's Breakfast', etc.: *When We Were Very Young*, Milne, A. A. (Methuen).

YOUNGER JUNIORS

'Chick', Stephens, J.,
'Dobbin', Noyes, A.,
'Windy Nights', Bennett, R.,
'Long, Long Ago', Anon.,
'Cats', Farjeon, E.: *Blackwell Junior Poetry*, Books 1 and 2 (Blackwell).
'The Frog', Belloc, H.,
'Five Eyes', De la Mare, W.,
'My Shadow', Stevenson, R. L.: *Book of Nursery Verse* (Faber).
'A Child's Song in Spring', Nesbitt, E.,
'The Crow', Alexander, C. F.,
'Danny Murphy', Stevens, J.,
'Duck's Ditty', Grahame, K.,
'The Elephant', Belloc, H.,
'From a Railway Carriage', Stevenson, R. L.,
'How Far is it to Bethlehem?', Chesterton, F.,
'Roadways', Masefield, J.: *Come Follow Me* (Evans).
'The Old Sailor',: *Now We Are Six*, Milne, A. A. (Methuen).
'Full Moon',
'Sooeep!',
'The Scarecrow', *Peacock Pie*, De la Mare (Faber & Faber).
'The Pied Piper', Browning, R.: *The Echoing Green*, Book 1 (Blackwell).
'The Wind in a Frolic', Howitt, W.: *The Merry Go Round* (Heinemann).
'Mr Nobody', Anon.,
'The Cow', Stevenson, R. L.: *The Merry Minstrel*, Book 1 (Blackie).
'We Be the King's Men', Hardy, T.,
'What is Pink?', Rossetti, C.,
'New Shoes', Brahems, C.,
'The Elephant', Asquith, A.: *The Merry Ministrel*, Book 2 (Blackie).
'Shoes and Stockings',
'Bad Sir Brian Botany',
'At the Zoo': *When We Were Very Young*, Milne, A. A. (Methuen).

OLDER JUNIORS

'How They Brought the Good News', Browning, R.: *A Wealth of Poetry* (Blackwell).
'Cargoes', Masefield, J.: *An Anthology of Modern Verse* (Methuen).
'The Wraggle Taggle Gipsies', Anon.: *Book of Children's Verse* (Faber).
'The Jumblies', Lear, E.: *Book of Nursery Verse* (Faber).
'The Pedlar's Caravan', Rands, W. B.,
'Rain', Davies, W. H.,
'The Highwayman', Noyes, A.,
'Sherwood', Noyes, A.: *Come Follow Me* (Evans).
'School's Out', Davies, W. H.: *Modern Verses* (Oxford U.P.).
'Shimbleshanks the Railway Cat': *Old Possum's Book of Practical Cats*, Eliot, T. S. (Faber).
'Meg Merrilees', Keats, J.,
'Song', Keats, J.,
'The Eagle', Tennyson, A. L.,
'The Brook', Tennyson, A. L.: *Oxford Book of Poetry for Children* (Oxford U.P.).
'The Fly', De la Mare, W.,
'Windy Nights', Stevenson, R. L.: *Oxford Book of Verse for Juniors*, Book 1 (Oxford U.P.).
'The Oxen', Hardy, T.: *Oxford Book of Verse for Juniors*, Book 3 (Oxford U.P.).
'The Wind in a Frolic', Howitt, W.: *The Merry Go Round* (Heinemann).
'The Pedlar's Caravan', Rands, W. B.,
'Little Billie', Thackeray, W. M.: *The Merry Minstrel*, Book 3 (Blackie).
'The Windmill', Longfellow, H. W.,
'Leisure', Davies, W. M.,
'Winter', Shakespeare, W.,
'The Sage's Pigtail', Thackeray, W. M.: *The Merry Minstrel*, Book 4 (Blackie).

Appendix IV

Useful Books for Teaching Music

GENERAL

The Oxford School Music Book, Junior Series, Pupils' Books 1–4, Teachers' Manuals 1 and 11, Fiske, R. and Dobbs, J. P. B. (Oxford U.P.).
Music Together, Winters, G. (Longmans).
Listening Together, Eele, M. (Novello).
Music in Schools, Education Pamphlet No. 27 (H.M.S.O.).

STORIES

The Sorcerer's Apprentice and Other Stories, Hosier, J. (Oxford U.P.). *The Nutcracker and Swan Lake*, Appleby, W. and Fowler, F. (Oxford U.P.).
The Sleeping Beauty and The Firebird, Appleby, W. and Fowler, F. (Oxford U.P.).
The Golden Cockerel, Gibson, E. (Oxford U.P.).

RECORDERS

The School Recorder, Books 1 and 2, (and the Book of Piano Accompaniments), Priestly, E. and Fowler (Arnold).
Play the Recorder, Books 1 and 2 (Graded Series), Salkeld, R. (Chappell).

CHRISTMAS MUSIC

Oxford Book of Carols for Schools (Oxford U.P.).
Carols with Chimes, Rees, O. and Mendoza, A. (Oxford U.P.).
More Carols with Chimes, Rees, O. and Mendoza, A. (Oxford U.P.).
Clarendon Books of Christmas Carols and Songs, Book 1, ed. Wiseman, H. and Northcote, S. (Oxford U.P.).
The Treasury of Christmas Music, ed. Reed, W. L. (Blandford).

INSTRUMENTS

Instruments of the Orchestra, Hosier, J. (Oxford, U.P.).
Ladybird Book of Musical Instruments, (Wills & Hepworth).
Set of pictures showing various instruments of the orchestra, Boosey and Hawkes, 295 Regent Street, London W1A 1BC.
Small pictures of musical instruments may be found in the *Oxford School Music Books*.

Appendix V

Suggestions for Further Reading

ADVICE FOR THE NEW TEACHER

Davies, W. T. and Shepherd, T. B., *Teaching: Begin Here* (Epworth, 1961).

Edmonds, E. L., *The First Year of Teaching* (London, N.U.T., 1967).

Edmonds, E. L., *Treasure Chest for Teachers* (Schoolmaster Pub. Co., 1967).

Palmer, F. C., *Student Guidance*, Education Today Series (Longmans, 1965).

Peterson, A. D. (ed.), *Technique of Teaching*, 3 vols (Pergaman, 1965).

ENGLISH

Cass, J. E., *Literature and the Young Child* (Longmans, 1967).

Clarke, E., *Stories to Tell and How to Tell Them* (Univ. Lond. Press).

Clegg, A. B., *The Excitement of Writing* (Chatto Windus, 1964).

Cutforth, J. A. and Battersby, S. H., *Children and Books* (Blackwell, 1962).

Daniels, and Diack, *The Standard Reading Tests* (Chatto & Windus, 1958).

Derrick, J., *Teaching English to Immigrants* (Longmans, 1966).

Goddard, N. L., *Reading in the Modern Infants School* (Univ. Lond. Press, 1969).

Hughes, J. M., *Aids to Reading* (Evans, 1970).

Lane, S. M. and Kemp, M., *An Approach to Creative Writing in the Primary School* (Blackie, 1967).

Mackay, D., Thompson, B. and Schaub, P. (for Schools Council), 'Break Through to Literacy', *Teachers' Manual* (Longman, 1970).

Maybury, B., *Creative Writing for Juniors* (Batsford, 1967).

Morgan, D. L., *Living Speech in the Primary School*, Education Today Series (Longmans, 1966).

Morris, H., *Where's That Poem?* (Blackwell, 1970).

Neale, M. D., *Analysis of Reading Ability* (Macmillan, 1958).
Slade, P., *An Introduction to Child Drama* (Univ. Land. Press, 1969).
Tansley, A. E., *Reading and Remedial Reading* (Routledge, 1967).
Turnbull, M. and Warwick, P., *Speak, Move and Act*, Books 1 and 2 (Hulton Ed., 1960).
Way, B., *Development Through Drama* (Longmans, 1967).

ABOUT CHILDREN'S BOOKS

Fisher, M., *Intent Upon Reading* (Brockhampton, 1961).
Green, R. L., *Tellers of Tales* (Kaye & Ward, 1946, rev. 1969).
National Book League, *Education Book Guide* (Councils & Education Press Ltd, annually).
White, D. N., *About Books for Children* (Oxford U.P., 1946).

PROJECTS AND ENVIRONMENTAL STUDIES

Allen, G., *Social Studies in the Primary School* (Macmillan, 1960).
Kent, G., *Projects in the Primary School* (Batsford, 1968).
Philips, H. and McInnes, F. T. C., *Exploration in the Junior School* (Univ. Lond. Press, 1950, 2nd ed. 1967).
Watts, D. G., *Environmental Studies* (Routledge & Kegan Paul, 1969).

MATHEMATICS

Barnet, N. M. and others, *Juniors Learning Mathematics* (Ward Lock, 1956).
Churchill, E. M., *Counting and Measuring* (Routledge, 1961).
Marsh, L. G., *Children Explore Mathematics* (Black, 1967).
Mott, E. M., *First Steps in Number Work* (Evans, 1961).
Schools Council, 'Mathematics in Primary Schools', *Curriculum Bulletin*, No. 1 (H.M.S.O., 1969).
Sealey, L. G. W., *The Creative Use of Mathematics in the Junior School* (Blackwell, 1961).
Stern, C., 'Children Discover Arithmetic', *Manual of Practical Considerations* (Harrap, 1953).
—— Nuffield Mathematics Project Books (Chambers/Murray, 1967).

SCIENCE

Nuffield Junior Science, *Source Books of Information*, Teachers' Background Booklets (Collins, 1967).

Schools Council, Nuffield Foundation and Scottish Education Dept, *Science 5–13 Units for Teachers* (Macdonald, 1967).

UNESCO, *Source Book for Science Teaching* (Educational Productions Ltd, 1966).

ART AND CRAFT

Dimmack, M., *A Dictionary of Creative Activities for School Use* (Macmillan, 1966).

Jameson, K., *Pre-School and Infant Art* (Studio Vista, London, 1968).

Johnson, P., *Creating with Paper* (Nicholas Kaye Ltd, 1960).

Pluckrose, H., *The Art and Craft Book* (Evans, 1969).

Seville, R., *Beginning Arts and Crafts* (Evans, 1964).

P.E.

Bilborough, A. and Jones, P., *Physical Education in the Primary School*, 3rd edition (Univ. Lond. Press, 1963).

Churcher, B. *Physical Education for Teaching* (Allen & Unwin, 1971).

Johnson, F. J. M. and Trevor, M. D., *A Suggested Games Scheme for Juniors* (Blackwell, 1970).

Jordan, D., *Childhood and Movement* (Blackwell, 1966).

Russell, J., *Creative Dance in the Primary School* (Macdonald & Evans, 1965).

GENERAL

—— 'Children and their Primary Schools' (Plowden Report) (H.M.S.O., 1967).

Ash, B. and Rapaport, B., *Skills in the Junior School* (Methuen, 1960).

Blackie, J., *Inside the Primary School* (H.M.S.O., 1967).

Gardner, D. E. M., *The Education of Young Children* (Methuen, 1956).

Gesell, A. and Ilg, F., *The Child from Five to Ten* (Hamish Hamilton, 1946).

Isaacs, S., *Intellectual Growth in Young Children* (Routledge, 1930).

Mellor, E., *Education through Experience in the Infant School Years* (Blackwell, 1950).

Peel, E. A., *The Psychological Basis of Education* (Oliver & Boyd, 1956).

Phelps, R., *Display in the Classroom* (Blackwell, 1969).

Ridgway L. and Lawton, I., *Family Grouping in the Infants School* (Ward Lock).

Sealey, L. G. W. and Gibbon, V., *Communication and Learning in the Primary School* (Blackwell, 1963).

Taylor, J., *Organizing and Integrating the Infant Day* (Allen & Unwin, 1971).

Vernon, P. E., *Measurement of Abilities* (U.L.P., 1940).

Williams, A. A., *Basic Subjects for the Slow Learner* (Methuen, 1970).

Appendix VI

Sources of Some Useful Equipment

FILMS AND FILM-STRIPS

16mm Movie Films to Hire:

The Rank Organization, Rank Film Library, 1 Aintree Road, Perivale, Greenford, Middlesex.

I.C.I. Film Library, Thames House North, Millbank, London, S.W.1.

Unilever Film Library, Unilever House, Blackfriars, London, E.C.4.

Petroleum Films Bureau, 4 Brook Street, London, W.1.

Sound-Services Ltd, Kingston Road, Merton Park, London, S.W. 19.

Dunlop Film Library, Wilton Crescent, Merton Park, London, S.W.19.

Religious Films Ltd, 6 Eaton Gate, London, S.W.1.

The Gas Council Film Library, 4/5 Grosvenor Place, London, S.W.1.

The British Railways Board, 25 Sackville Row, London, W.1.

The Gateway Film Theatre Productions, E.F.V.A., 35 Queen Anne Street, London, W.1.

British Transport Films, 25 Savile Row, London, W.1.

National Coal Board, 26–28 Dorset Square, London, N.W.1.

35mm Film-Strips to Buy:

Concordia Film, Concordia House, 117/123 Golden Lane, London, E.C.1.

Common Ground (1951) Ltd, 44 Fulham Road, London. S.W.3.

Visual Publications Ltd, 197 Kensington High Street, London, W.8.

Ladybird Film-Strips Library, Wills & Hepworth Ltd, Loughborough, Leicestershire.

Educational Productions Ltd, East Ardsley, Wakefield, Yorkshire, or 17 Denbigh Street, London. S.W.1.

Movie Films, Film-Strips and Slides to Borrow or Buy:

Foundation Film Library, Brooklands House, Weybridge, Surrey.
Photographs:
Aerofilms Ltd, 4 Albemarle Street, London, W.1.

WALL CHARTS AND OTHER INFORMATION

Schoolmaster Publishing Co., Hamilton House, Hastings Street, London, W.C.1 (for the booklet *Treasure Chest for Teachers*).
Educational Productions Ltd, East Ardsley, Wakefield, Yorkshire, or 17 Denbigh Street, London, S.W.1.
Brooke Bond Tea Co. Ltd, Education Dept, 35–37 Cannon Street, London, E.C.4.
British Trades Alphabet, Lofthouse, Wakefield, Yorkshire.
Cadbury Brothers Ltd, Schools Dept, Bournville, Birmingham 30.
Gas Council, 1 Grosvenor Place, London, S.W.1.
International Wool Secretariat, Department of Education, Dorland House, 18 Regent Street, London, S.W.1.
Dunlop Rubber Co. Ltd, 10 King Street, St James's, London, S.W.1.
National Milk Publicity Council, Melbourne House, Aldwych, London, W.C.2.
Pictorial Charts Unit, 181 Uxbridge Road, Hanwell, London, W.7.
Visual Aids Centre, 78 High Holborn, London, W.C.1.

TRANSPARENT BOOK COVERS

Storeys, Lancaster, for 'Contact' adhesive, obtainable through usual educational suppliers.

RECORDS FOR MOVEMENT AND DANCE

'Carnival of Animals', Saint-Saëns
'Coppélia', Délibes
'Danse Macabre', Saint-Saëns
'English Folk Songs Suite', Vaughan Williams
'Fantasia on Greensleeves', Vaughan Williams
'L'Arlésienne Suite', Bizet
'Listen, Move and Dance' H.M.V. 7 EG 8727, 8728, 8762
'Night on the Bare Mountain', Mussorgsky
'Nutcracker Suite', Tschaikovsky
Orpheus in the Underworld, Offenbach
'Peer Gynt Suite', Grieg

'Peter and the Wolf', Prokofiev
Rosamunde (Incidental Music from), Schubert
'The Sleeping Beauty' (selections), Tschaikovsky
'The Sorcerer's Apprentice', Dukas
'Tritsch-Tratsch Polka', Strauss
William Tell (Overture to Act 3), Rossini

and numerous others.

EMI Records, EMI House, 20 Manchester Square, London, W1A 1ES, will send to schools lists of recorded music suitable for use in primary schools.

Index